risotto

risotto

with vegetables, seafood, meat, and more

Maxine Clark

photography by Martin Brigdale

RYLAND
PETERS
& SMALL

LONDON NEW YORK

First published in the United States in 2005

This paperback edition published
by Ryland Peters & Small, Inc. in 2009
519 Broadway, 5th Floor
New York, NY 10012
www.rylandpeters.com

10 9 8 7 6 5 4 3 2 1

ISBN: 978 1 84597 809 9

The original hardcover edition is cataloged
as follows:

Library of Congress
Cataloging-in-Publication Data

Clark, Maxine.
  Risotto with vegetables, seafood, meat, and
more / Maxine Clark ; photography by Martin
Brigdale.
    p. cm.
  Includes index.
  ISBN-10: 1-84172-812-8
  ISBN-13: 978-1-84172-812-4
  1. Cookery (Rice) 2. Risotto. 3. Cookery,
Italian. I. Title.
  TX809.R5C53 2005
  641.6'318--dc22
                       2004014645

Printed and bound in China.

Dedication

I dedicate this book to my friend Pia Scavia,
a Milanese who is both inspirational and stoic
and doesn't mind using a bouillon cube.

Acknowledgments

My thanks go to all at RPS; Elsa and Alison for
encouraging me to write this book and Steve
for his patience at the studio, his good design,
and enthusiastic risotto tasting. Martin has yet
again produced beautiful, natural looking
photographs with a subject that is difficult to
control. Helen supplied us with evocative yet
calm props and backgrounds. My thanks to
Bridget, for producing some beautiful risottos.
Belinda Spinney ably assisted me in the kitchen
and will probably never want to see rice in any
form again. Thanks too must go to Silvia
Brugiamolini at Esperya for dealing with my
large rice order so efficiently—the rice was a
treat to use. I would like to add my thanks to
Antonietta Kelly at the Italian Trade Commission
for supplying information from The Italian
Association of Rice Producers. My thanks also
to Nowelle Valentino-Capezza for her help with
the translations.

Senior Designer Steve Painter
Commissioning Editor
              Elsa Petersen-Schepelern
Editor Susan Stuck
Art Director Gabriella Le Grazie
Publishing Director Alison Starling

Food Stylists Maxine Clark,
              Bridget Sargeson
Prop Stylist Helen Trent
Indexer Hilary Bird

Notes

- All spoon measurements are level unless
otherwise stated.
- All herbs are fresh, unless specified
otherwise.
- Ingredients in this book are available from
larger supermarkets and Italian food markets.
See page 142 for mail order sources.
- Eggs are large unless otherwise specified.
Uncooked or partially cooked eggs should not
be served to the very old, the frail, young
children, pregnant women, or those with
compromised immune systems.

contents

6 calming, sensuous, satisfying ...
10 the basics
22 vegetables
60 cheese and eggs
76 poultry and game
90 meat and bacon
104 fish and seafood
126 other ways with risotto
142 websites and mail order
143 index

Making a risotto is one of the most calming, sensuous, satisfying cooking experiences I know. Make it in a hurry at your peril—this is a dish to be made after a hard day, while you're winding down with a glass of wine. Though the cooking process takes only about 30 minutes from beginning to end, it's best to do all the preparation and chopping before you start cooking the rice. Have the stock ready and keep it hot over very gentle heat while you make the risotto.

There are no sudden movements when risotto-making. The butter is melted very gently; the vegetables are added and slowly cooked in their own juices until soft. The rice is stirred in and pan-toasted until it smells vaguely nutty, then the wine is splashed in "with a sigh." The broth is gently ladled in, sighing again each time. Then the rice is stirred languorously to encourage the starch to leave the outside of the grains and thicken the sauce. The bubbles in the liquid move and burst slowly. The rice should always look voluptuous and never be allowed to dry out.

Almost anything can be cooked into a risotto—and it can be added right at the beginning before the rice if it should be cooked for longer than 12–20 minutes, or it can be stirred in at the end. Traditional methods of cooking vegetable risottos like asparagus involve adding the vegetables early so they disintegrate into the risotto, cooking and sealing the flavor into the creaminess of the dish. It is now more fashionable to stir in precooked vegetables to give a contrast between mild, creamy rice and the added ingredient. But it is all a matter of taste. People get very wound up about whether a risotto should be soupy and very firm, others like it creamy and thick. Ignore what people say and cook it as you like it. Just don't overcook it to a mushy porridge—that is unkind to the rice as well as your taste buds.

ingredients and utensils

The cultivation of rice in Italy
The cultivation of rice is as ancient as the making of wine and olive oil, thus providing a staple on which people could survive. Italian rice has its genetic roots in the original species *Oryza sativa,* a member of the Gramineae or grass family, the *japonica* subspecies of which was probably brought to Europe through Arab expansion into the Mediterranean basin. It was probably known before this time, arriving via the busy trade routes with the Middle and Far East, where it had

been cultivated for thousands of years. The *japonica* has a higher starch content than the other most important subspecies, *indica.*

Italian rice cultivation is concentrated in the Po Valley in northern Italy (Piedmont and Lombardy), but it is also grown around Venice, Emilia Romagna, Sardinia, and a little in Tuscany and Calabria. Rice production soared in the latter part of the nineteenth century after the development of manageable irrigation in Vercelli in Piedmont coupled with the invention of bigger and better rice-milling machinery. Vercelli is now the epicenter of rice-growing in Europe and has a rice stock exchange, the Borsa del Riso. New varieties have been developed since the singular variety simply called *nostrale* was consumed across Italy for over 400 years from the fifteenth century, so that more than 50 varieties are now available. Although rice is no longer considered a staple or "food of the poor," the average Italian still consumes about 10 pounds of rice per year: in the late 19th century, it was more than double that amount. Rice is planted in flooded fields in March, and takes 180 days to grow and finally ripen for harvest in October. Until 40 years ago, rice was still picked by hand, but now it is gathered by huge combine harvesters. It is reaped, threshed, and dried, then sold for milling and distribution. The milling process removes any dust, immature grains, and the outer husk. Then it is polished to remove a second "sheath" and the broken grains removed from the whole ones. Some rice is still polished *all'antica* (in the old way) using stone pestles (*lavorato con pestelli*) that give the grain a coarser, more rustic appearance and a little more fiber.

Which Italian risotto rice is best?
There are three varieties readily available around the world: arborio, carnaroli, and vialone nano—these are the best for making risotto. In general, I like to use carnaroli or vialone nano, with arborio last though not least favorite. Arborio is the most popular variety of short-grain risotto rice. It has a lightly higher "stickiness" or starch rating which makes it good for timbales and very creamy risottos. Personally, I think that arborio can become too mushy too quickly, whereas carnaroli has wonderful absorption, releases enough starch to make the risotto creamy and not sticky, and the grains still remain firm—*al dente.* Carnaroli is the rice preferred by most Italian cooks. Vialone nano has a shorter grain, a good absorption when cooked, and is another rice with low stickiness or starch. This is preferred in the Veneto and Mantova in Lombardy for traditional recipes that require a looser risotto with a firm grain. Other newer risotto

varieties available in Italy are *baldo* and *Roma,* which are both high in starch and make very creamy risottos and good timbales. There are many other types of rice, but not all are suitable for risotto making.

Italian rice is divided into four group classifications by law; *originario or comune, semifino, fino,* and *superfino.* This doesn't denote quality or "cookability," but length, appearance, and shape. Every package should display the group and variety.

Can I use another rice instead of Italian risotto rice?

No. Rice suitable for risotto has a "pearl" in the center of the grain. On inspection, you will clearly see that the center is whiter than the edges. This opaque central zone is made up of a farinaceous starch that is different from the starch on the outside of the grain. During cooking the outside starch dissolves into the liquid when the rice is stirred or beaten, while the interior starch absorbs liquid and swells. *Indica* rices such as basmati, Thai jasmine, and American long-grain rice do not have this "pearl" in the center. Therefore, Italian risotto rice is the only rice with the right makeup to absorb a large amount of liquid, release starch as it is stirred to make a creamy sauce, yet retain the shape and firmness of the grain without disintegrating and becoming gluey. Risotto is never gluey—it is always moist and creamy.

How do I store rice?

Rice absorbs moisture and odors, so store it like wine in a cool, dry, airy place. I keep it in an airtight storage jar well away from the oven or stove-top. If you like the look of the packaging, put the whole thing into a glass preserving jar with a rubber seal, close, and admire!

What is *al dente?*

This means that the center of the grain of rice is still firm to the bite, but cooked and definitely not mushy. It still has some delicate resistance. Some (especially the Venetians) say that the rice should still be a little gritty or chalky in the center, but this is personal and I do not like it like that. You can take this *al dente* business too far.

Butter—salted or unsalted?

Always unsalted—it gives a purer, sweeter flavor.

Real broth or bouillon cubes?

Ideally, real broth is better, as it is the heart of the risotto, but it must not be too strong. Realistically, most Italians would use a bouillon cube to make an everyday risotto, but they are lucky to have quite a choice available and I think that their cubes are of a better quality than those available elsewhere. *Gusto Classico* is a good all-round flavor—it is light and suitable for meat or poultry dishes.

How much broth?

As much as the rice will take. Always have more broth ready than the recipe states—you never know how much that particular rice will absorb on that particular day. It depends on how fast the rice is bubbling (too fast and the broth evaporates instead of being absorbed into the rice) and the type of pan you use.

Which pan to use?

A medium to large shallow pan (but not like a skillet) with a heavy base. Enameled cast iron or heavy stainless steel with a sandwiched base are good. I have a deep, heavy-gauge, aluminum sauté pan, perfect for risotto-making. A thin, flimsy pan is not suitable—the rice will stick and burn and you will not be able to control the simmer. Use too wide or shallow a pan, and the broth will evaporate too quickly and concentrate its flavor too much into the rice. Too deep and the rice will take ages to cook—it will stew and become mushy. All in all, a heavy saucepan that is not too deep is the answer. Make sure it is big enough to enable you to stir comfortably and for the rice to swell.

Parmigiano Reggiano or bust!

You do not have to use real Parmigiano Reggiano for risotto all the time. Parmigiano is a hard *grana* cheese with a D.O.P. status (*Denominazione d'Origine Protetta*), which promotes the authenticity and artisan characteristics of certain food and agricultural products—this one can come only from the provinces of Modena, Reggio Emilia, Parma, and part of Bologna and Mantua, and is made in a particular way. Grana Padano D.O.P. is a less expensive *grana* cheese made in the Po Valley, and is perfectly acceptable to stir into a risotto. Fresh *grana* should smell sweet and nutty—never use the stuff found in the round cardboard canister. Extra cheese is not generally served with a fish or seafood risotto, the one exception being black squid ink risotto (page 107).

To shave or not to shave …

Personally, I don't like shaved Parmesan on a risotto—it sticks to the rice like a soggy blanket and the heat makes it floppy and greasy. I prefer the cheese finely grated almost to a powder, so it will melt smoothly into the rice. However, I do like it shaved over salads, where the cheese is actually an element of the dish.

the basics

white risotto step by step
risotto in bianco

This is the method for a basic, unflavored risotto without cheese. The method always remains the same, but the ingredients change slightly. Sometimes, instead of plain onion, a *soffritto*–a finely chopped mixture of onion, carrot, and celery–can delicately flavor the base of a risotto. Cubed pancetta or prosciutto is sometimes added at this stage, but must not be allowed to brown or it will become tough. Although the stated amount of broth is correct, I like to top it up to 2 quarts just in case the rice becomes too thick (you could use hot water instead). The important thing is not to rush making a risotto–treat it with love and respect and you will achieve perfect results.

Note This recipe gives 4 very generous entrée servings or 6 smaller servings. Allow about ½ cup of rice per person for a generous serving, but less if adding a lot of meat or vegetables.

about 6 cups hot Light Chicken Broth (page 16) or Vegetable Broth (page 15)

1 stick unsalted butter

1 onion, finely chopped

2 cups risotto rice

⅔ cup dry white wine (optional)

sea salt and freshly ground black pepper

Serves 4–6

white risotto step-by-step
risotto in bianco

1

Put the broth in a saucepan and keep at a gentle simmer. Melt half the butter in a large, heavy saucepan and add the onion. Cook gently for 10 minutes until soft, golden, and translucent but not browned.

2

Add the rice and stir until well coated with butter and heated through (this is called the *tostatura* and the rice should start to crackle slightly).

3

Pour in the wine, if using—you should hear a "sigh" (*sospiro*) as it is added. Boil hard until it has reduced and almost disappeared. This will remove the taste of raw alcohol.

4

Begin adding the broth, a large ladle at a time, stirring gently until each ladle has been almost absorbed into the rice. The risotto should be kept at a bare simmer throughout cooking, so don't let the rice dry out—add more broth as necessary. Continue until the rice is tender and creamy, but the grains still firm. This should take 15–20 minutes, depending on the type of rice used—check the package instructions.

5

Taste and season well with salt and pepper and beat in the remaining butter (this process of beating is called *mantecare*).

Note Sometimes, according to the recipe, grated Parmesan cheese is beaten in with the butter at this stage.

6

Cover and let rest for a couple of minutes so the risotto can relax and any cheese will melt, then serve immediately. Venetians believe risotto should be served *al onda* (like a wave), referring to its liquid texture—so you may like to add a little more hot broth just before you serve to loosen it, but don't let the risotto wait too long or the rice will turn mushy.

Too many vegetable broths are insipid or taste of a single ingredient. This broth is extravagant in its use of vegetables, but will have very good flavor. Broth gives a risotto body and depth of flavor, but shouldn't dominate the dish. Strong root vegetables such as turnips and parsnips are not good additions, and neither are potatoes or cabbage. Although you should always use the best and freshest ingredients, you can use bits and pieces lurking in the vegetable bin of the refrigerator. Remember to wash everything first or you will end up with gritty broth. If you want a stronger broth, just strain, then boil hard to reduce it.

vegetable broth

brodo vegetale

1 large onion, quartered

2 large carrots, quartered

1 small bunch of celery, coarsely chopped (leaves and all)

2 leeks, white parts only, halved lengthwise, rinsed and halved again

4 zucchini, thickly sliced

2 tomatoes, halved around the middle and seeds squeezed out

1 fennel bulb, quartered

1 romaine lettuce heart, coarsely chopped

3 garlic cloves

1 dried red chile

4 fresh bay leaves

a handful of parsley stalks, crushed

½ lemon, sliced

6 black peppercorns

salt, to taste

Makes 2–3 quarts

Put all the ingredients in a large soup kettle. Add water to cover, about 4 quarts, and bring to a boil. Reduce the heat as soon as it is boiling and simmer for 15 minutes. Stir the broth and skim, then cook at the barest simmer for 1 hour, skimming often.

Remove from the heat and strain the broth into a bowl through a colander lined with cheesecloth. Discard the contents of the colander after they have cooled. Cool the broth and refrigerate for several hours.

At this stage you can reboil the broth to concentrate it, or cover and refrigerate or freeze until needed. The broth will keep in the refrigerator for 3 days or frozen for up to 6 months.

light chicken broth
brodo di pollo

Although Italians are not shy of using bouillon cubes (*dadi di brodo*), a good broth is worth making and can add real depth of flavor to a risotto. It is important not to make the broth too concentrated or dark in color—it mustn't mask the true flavors in the risotto. You can make the broth using a whole chicken instead of chicken wings if you like, but I think this is sometimes a waste and chicken wings are flavorsome and give a good jellied broth.

3½ lb. chicken wings

2 carrots, coarsely chopped

2 onions, coarsely chopped

1 whole small bunch of celery including any leaves, trimmed, coarsely chopped, then washed

1 large fresh bouquet garni (bay leaves, thyme, rosemary, and parsley stalks, tied up with kitchen twine)

a few black peppercorns

Makes 2–3 quarts

Cut the chicken wings into pieces through their joints. Put these into a large soup kettle with the carrots, onions, celery, bouquet garni, and peppercorns. Add water to cover, about 4 quarts, and bring to a boil. As soon as it is boiling, reduce to a simmer, stir and skim, then continue to cook at the barest simmer for 3 hours, skimming often. Remove from the heat and strain the broth into a bowl through a colander lined with cheesecloth.

When cool, discard the contents of the colander. Cool the broth and refrigerate for several hours. Remove from the refrigerator and lift off any fat that has set on top of the jellied broth. At this stage you can reboil the broth to concentrate it, or cover and refrigerate or freeze until needed. This stock will keep in the refrigerator for about 3–4 days or in the freezer for up to 6 months.

game broth
brodo di cacciagione

For a rich, full flavor, the carcasses are browned before simmering with the vegetables. To make it darker, add the onion skins with the vegetables. If making duck broth, render the skin over medium heat to release the fat, then add the carcasses and brown them all over. Duck fat contains lots of flavor—skim the fat off later when the broth has cooled and set.

4 tablespoons unsalted butter

2 lb. carcasses (plus any cleaned giblets, except the liver) of feathered game, chopped

1 onion, chopped

1 leek, split, washed, and chopped

1 carrot, chopped

2 celery stalks, chopped

a few fresh parsley stalks, lightly crushed

6 black peppercorns

a pinch of salt

Makes about 2 quarts

Melt the butter in a large soup kettle. When foaming, add the carcasses and sauté over low heat until light brown and on no account burnt. Add all the remaining ingredients and stir well. Add water to cover, about 3 quarts, and bring to a boil. Reduce to a simmer, stir, and skim the surface, then continue to cook at the barest simmer for 2 hours, skimming often. Remove from the heat and strain the broth into a bowl through a colander lined with cheesecloth.

When cool, discard the contents of the colander. Cool the broth and refrigerate for several hours. Remove from the refrigerator and lift off any fat that has set on top of the jellied broth. At this stage you can reboil the broth to concentrate it, or cover and refrigerate or freeze until needed. This broth will keep in the refrigerator for about 3–4 days or in the freezer for up to 6 months.

I like to use a light meat broth for making risotto, so I don't brown the meat, bones, or vegetables before simmering. My broth has body and is well flavored. However, if you prefer a richer broth, brown the bones in a hot oven and, while they are browning, sauté the meat and vegetables in the soup kettle until they are a good red-brown, but do not let them over-brown or they will give the broth a bitter taste. If you don't have access to bones (these do give a great deal of body to the broth), add the same weight of beef or veal with good amounts of connective tissue—such as you find in inexpensive, tough cuts.

beef or veal broth

brodo di manzo o vitello

2 lb. stewing beef or veal or brisket

1 lb. beef or veal bones

1 onion, coarsely chopped

2 carrots, coarsely chopped

2 leeks, split, washed, and chopped

2 celery stalks, coarsely chopped

a few parsley stalks, lightly crushed

2 bay leaves

6 whole black peppercorns

a pinch of salt

Makes 2–3 quarts

Put all the ingredients in a large soup kettle. Add enough water to cover, about 4 quarts, and bring to a boil. Reduce the heat as soon as it is boiling, stir, and skim the surface, then continue to cook at the barest simmer for 3 hours, skimming often.

Remove from the heat and strain the broth into a bowl through a colander lined with cheesecloth. Discard the contents of the colander when they have cooled. Cool the broth, then refrigerate for several hours. Remove from the refrigerator and lift off any fat that has set on top of the jellied broth.

At this stage you can reboil the broth to concentrate it, or cover and refrigerate or freeze until needed. This broth will keep in the refrigerator for about 3–4 days or in the freezer for up to 6 months.

Variation Game Broth with Venison
When a recipe calls for game broth, make the recipe above, using wild boar or venison meat and bones (or veal bones), or use beef broth instead.

fish broth

brodo di pesce

Use trimmings (skin) and bones left from filleting white fish such as sole, cod, or haddock. Oily fish like salmon, sardines, and mackerel should be avoided (they are too strong in flavor). I simmer the vegetables before adding the fish trimmings and bones. This will extract more flavor, because if the fish is cooked longer than 20 minutes, the broth will be bitter.

1 leek, split, washed, and chopped

2 celery stalks, coarsely chopped

1 carrot, coarsely chopped

a few parsley stalks, lightly crushed

2 fresh bay leaves

3 thick lemon slices

4 black peppercorns and a good pinch of salt

½ cup dry white wine

3 lb. white fish trimmings and bones, chopped

Makes 2–3 quarts

Put all the ingredients except the fish trimmings and bones in a large soup kettle. Add water to cover, about 4 quarts, and bring to a boil. Reduce the heat as soon as it is boiling and simmer for 15 minutes. Stir the broth and skim, then add the fish trimmings and bones. Slowly return to a boil, then reduce the heat and cook at the barest simmer for 20 minutes, skimming often.

Remove from the heat and strain the broth into a bowl through a colander lined with cheesecloth. Discard the contents of the colander when they have cooled. Cool the broth, then refrigerate for several hours, when it should set to a jelly.

At this stage you can reboil the broth to concentrate it, or cover and refrigerate or freeze until needed. The broth will keep in the refrigerator for 2 days or frozen for up to 3 months.

quick seafood broth

brodo leggero di frutti di mare

Although a light fish broth will do, this is a good way to use up any shrimp heads or shells, crab, or lobster shells you would usually throw away. This broth is quite sweet, unlike a broth made with white fish.

1 onion or ½ leek, chopped

1 celery stalk with leaves, coarsely chopped

a few parsley stalks, lightly crushed

2 bay leaves

2 slices of lemon

4 black peppercorns

¼ cup dry white wine

a good pinch of salt

2 lb. mixture of seafood pieces (shrimp heads or cheap shrimp, crab, lobster, or crawfish shells)

Makes 2 quarts

Put all the ingredients except the seafood pieces in a large soup kettle. Add water to cover, about 3 quarts, and bring to a boil. As soon as it boils, reduce the heat and simmer for 15 minutes. Stir the broth and skim, then add the seafood pieces. Slowly return to a boil, then reduce the heat and cook at the barest simmer for 20 minutes, skimming often.

Remove from the heat and strain the broth into a bowl through a colander lined with cheesecloth. Discard the contents of the colander when they have cooled. Cool the broth and refrigerate for several hours.

At this stage you can reboil the broth to concentrate it, or cover and refrigerate or freeze until needed. The broth will keep in the refrigerator for 1–2 days or frozen for up to 3 months.

vegetables

Stirring in real, homemade pesto just before you eat this risotto makes it taste heavenly—quite an explosion on the taste buds. This recipe makes a thick pesto: if you prefer the idea of a lake of pesto floating over the surface of the risotto, then simply add more olive oil to the mixture. To make good pesto, you must use the right weight of very fresh basil leaves—too little basil and it will taste insipid.

pesto risotto
risotto al pesto

about 6 cups hot Light Chicken Broth (page 16) or Vegetable Broth (page 15)

1 stick unsalted butter

1 onion, finely chopped

2⅓ cups risotto rice

⅔ cup dry white wine (optional)

sea salt and freshly ground black pepper

pesto genovese

2 garlic cloves

½ cup pine nuts

1¼ cups chopped fresh basil leaves

⅔ cup extra virgin olive oil (or more)

4 tablespoons unsalted butter, softened

¼ cup freshly grated Parmesan cheese

sea salt and freshly ground black pepper

Serves 6

To make the pesto, use a mortar and pestle to pound the garlic to a cream with a little salt. Add the pine nuts and pound thoroughly. Add the basil leaves a few at a time, pounding and mixing to a paste. Gradually beat in the olive oil until the mixture is creamy and thick. Beat in the butter and season with pepper, then beat in the cheese. Store in a glass bottle, with a layer of olive oil on top to exclude the air, in the refrigerator until needed. Alternatively, put everything in a blender or food processor and blend until smooth.

Put the broth in a saucepan and keep at a gentle simmer. Melt half the butter in a large, heavy saucepan and add the onion. Cook gently for 10 minutes until soft, golden, and translucent but not browned. Add the rice and stir until well coated with butter and heated through. Add the wine, if using, and boil hard until it has reduced and almost disappeared. This will remove the taste of raw alcohol.

Begin adding the broth, a large ladle at a time, stirring gently until each one has been almost absorbed into the rice. The risotto should be kept at a bare simmer throughout cooking, so don't let the rice dry out—add more broth as necessary. Continue until the rice is tender and creamy, but the grains still firm. (This should take 15–20 minutes, depending on the type of rice used—check the package instructions.) Taste and season well with salt and pepper, then beat in the remaining butter.

Cover and let rest for a couple of minutes so the risotto can relax, then serve immediately. You may like to add a little more hot broth to the risotto just before you serve to loosen it, but don't let it wait too long or the rice will turn mushy. Serve in warm bowls with a large spoonful of pesto in each or spoon liquid pesto over the entire surface before serving.

This simple risotto makes the most of young spinach and peppery arugula, but watercress makes a good alternative if you can't find arugula. Even if you hate anchovies, don't leave them out. They will dissolve into nothing, but add a salty, savory flavor to the heart of the risotto. If you are a vegetarian, you could add a dash of soy sauce to the broth instead.

spinach risotto
with arugula and roasted tomatoes
risotto con spinaci, rucola e pomodori

about 6 cups hot Vegetable Broth (page 15)

1 stick unsalted butter

1 onion, finely chopped

2 anchovies in oil

2 cups risotto rice

⅔ cup dry white wine

1 lb. baby plum tomatoes

¼ cup olive oil

8 oz. young fresh spinach leaves, washed and drained

2 cups fresh arugula leaves

sea salt and freshly ground black pepper

freshly grated Parmesan cheese, to serve

Serves 4

Put the broth in a saucepan and keep at a gentle simmer. Melt half the butter in a large, heavy saucepan and add the onion and anchovy. Cook gently for 10 minutes until soft, golden, and translucent but not browned. Add the rice and stir until well coated with the butter and heated through. Pour in the wine and boil hard to reduce until it has almost disappeared. This will remove the taste of raw alcohol. Remove from the heat.

Put the tomatoes in a roasting pan and sprinkle with olive oil. Mix well to coat, then season with salt and pepper. Roast in a preheated oven at 400°F for about 20 minutes or until slightly collapsed with the skins beginning to brown. Remove from the oven and set aside.

Return the risotto to the heat, warm through, and begin adding the broth, a large ladle at a time, stirring gently until each ladle has been almost absorbed into the rice. The risotto should be kept at a bare simmer throughout cooking, so don't let the rice dry out—add more broth as necessary. Continue until the rice is tender and creamy, but the grains still firm. (This should take between 15–20 minutes depending on the type of rice used—check the package instructions.) Just before the risotto is cooked, stir in the spinach and arugula. Taste and season well with salt and pepper, then beat in the remaining butter and Parmesan. You may like to add a little more hot broth at this stage to loosen the risotto.

Cover and let rest for a couple of minutes so the risotto can relax, the cheese melt, and the spinach and arugula wilt. Fold in the tomatoes and their juices, then serve immediately.

Tomato and rice soup at its best! The risotto is full of the intense flavor of tomatoes, added in three ways: passata to the broth; sun-dried tomatoes adding their caramel flavor deep in the risotto; then finally tiny ripe plum tomatoes, roasted to perfect sweetness. Delicious hot—but the leftovers are marvellous eaten straight out of the pan.

triple tomato risotto with basil
risotto ai tre pomodori

1 lb. whole baby plum tomatoes

¼ cup olive oil

about 1 quart hot Vegetable Broth (page 15)

2 cups passata (Italian puréed, strained tomatoes)

1 stick unsalted butter

1 onion, finely chopped

8 pieces sun-dried tomatoes (not the ones in oil), chopped

2 cups risotto rice, preferably vialone nano

⅔ cup light red wine

½ cup freshly grated Parmesan cheese

¼ cup chopped fresh basil

sea salt and freshly ground black pepper

to serve

extra basil leaves

freshly grated Parmesan cheese

Serves 4

Put the plum tomatoes in a roasting pan and pour over the olive oil. Mix well to coat and season with salt and pepper. Roast in a preheated oven at 400°F for about 20 minutes or until slightly collapsed and the skins are beginning to brown. Remove from the oven and set aside.

Pour the broth and passata into a saucepan, stir well, then heat to a gentle simmer. Melt half the butter in a large, heavy saucepan and add the onion and chopped sun-dried tomatoes. Cook gently for 10 minutes until soft, golden, and translucent but not browned. Add the rice and stir until well coated with the butter and heated through. Pour in the wine and boil hard until it has reduced and almost disappeared. This will remove the taste of raw alcohol. Remove from the heat.

Return the risotto to the heat, warm through, then begin adding the broth, a large ladle at a time, stirring gently until each ladle has almost been absorbed by the rice. The risotto should be kept at a bare simmer throughout cooking, so don't let the rice dry out—add more broth as necessary. Continue until the rice is tender and creamy, but the grains still firm (15–20 minutes depending on the type of rice used—check the package instructions).

Season to taste with salt and pepper and beat in the remaining butter, the Parmesan, and chopped basil. You may like to add a little more hot broth to the risotto at this stage to loosen it—it should be quite wet. Cover and let rest for a couple of minutes so the risotto can relax and the cheese melt. Carefully ladle into warm bowls and cover the surface with the roasted tomatoes and any juices. Add the basil leaves and serve immediately with extra freshly grated Parmesan cheese.

A spectacular risotto, full of earthy sweetness from finely cubed beets. Using raspberry vinegar instead of wine is a good tip, as long as you don't use too much. The raspberry complements the beets and the vinegar keeps the red onion nice and pink. I serve this topped with broiled radicchio and melting Fontina cheese for that contrast of sweet and bitter.

beet risotto
with broiled radicchio
risotto con barbabietole e radicchio arrostito

about 6 cups hot Vegetable Broth (page 15)

1 lb. raw beets, peeled and cut into small cubes

1 stick unsalted butter

1 red onion, finely chopped

3 tablespoons raspberry vinegar or red wine vinegar

2⅓ cups risotto rice

2 cups freshly grated Fontina cheese

3 tablespoons chopped fresh flat-leaf parsley

sea salt and freshly ground black pepper

broiled radicchio (optional)

3 small radicchio, quartered lengthwise

½ cup olive oil

Serves 6

Pour the broth into a saucepan and keep at a gentle simmer on top of the stove. Add the beets to the broth and simmer for 20–30 minutes until almost tender. Lift out the beets with a slotted spoon and set aside.

Melt half the butter in a large, heavy saucepan and add the onion and vinegar. Cook gently for 10 minutes until soft, golden, and translucent, but not browned. Add the cooked beets, then the rice, and stir until well coated with butter and heated through. Begin adding the broth, a large ladle at a time, stirring gently until each ladle has almost been absorbed by the rice. The risotto should be kept at a bare simmer throughout cooking, so don't let the rice dry out—add more broth as necessary. Continue until the rice is tender and creamy, but the grains still firm. (This should take 15–20 minutes depending on the type of rice used—check the package instructions.) Taste and season well with salt and pepper, then beat in the remaining butter, Fontina, and parsley. Cover and let rest for a couple of minutes so the risotto can relax and the cheese melt, then serve immediately. You may like to add a little more hot broth to the risotto just before you serve to loosen it, but don't let it wait around too long or the rice will turn mushy.

If serving with the radicchio, heat the broiler. Put the radicchio pieces in a broiler pan and brush with the oil. Broil for 10–15 minutes until soft and beginning to brown, turning a couple of times. Remove from the broiler and set aside. Stir half the Fontina into the risotto before resting. Ladle the risotto into 4 heatproof bowls and top each one with 2 radicchio quarters. Sprinkle with the remaining Fontina, set on a baking sheet and broil for 5 minutes until the cheese is melted and bubbling. Serve immediately.

I live in Scotland and was tempted to make a traditional pumpkin risotto using what we call "turnip" (rutabaga) instead. I was very impressed with the result. It was less sweet and cloying than it would be using pumpkin or squash, but had a most distinct flavor. This squash version tastes wonderful on its own or served with grilled lamb chops.

butternut squash, sage, and chile risotto

risotto alla zucca, salvia e peperoncino

about 6 cups hot Light Chicken Broth (page 16) or Vegetable Broth (page 15)

1 stick unsalted butter

1 large onion, finely chopped

1–2 fresh or dried red chiles, seeded and finely chopped

1 lb. fresh butternut squash or pumpkin (or rutabaga), peeled and finely chopped (2½ cups)

2⅓ cups risotto rice

3 tablespoons chopped fresh sage

¾ cup freshly grated Parmesan cheese

sea salt and freshly ground black pepper

Serves 6

Pour the broth into a saucepan and keep at a gentle simmer. Melt half the butter in a large, heavy saucepan and add the onion. Cook gently for 10 minutes until soft, golden, and translucent but not browned. Stir in the chopped chiles and cook for 1 minute. Add the butternut or pumpkin and cook, stirring constantly over the heat for 5 minutes, until it begins to soften slightly. Stir in the rice to coat with the butter and vegetables. Cook for a few minutes to toast the grains.

Begin adding the broth, a large ladle at a time, stirring gently until each ladle has almost been absorbed by the rice. The risotto should be kept at a bare simmer throughout cooking, so don't let the rice dry out—add more broth as necessary. Continue until the rice is tender and creamy, but the grains still firm and the squash or pumpkin beginning to disintegrate. (This should take about 15–20 minutes depending on the type of rice used—check the package instructions.)

Taste, season well with salt and pepper, and stir in the sage, remaining butter, and all the Parmesan. Cover, let rest for a couple of minutes, then serve.

A pretty orange color speckled with sweet green peas, this risotto is a delight to eat—the peas pop in your mouth and the seeds give crunch. Fresh peas in season are fantastic, but I am a fan of frozen peas and am never ashamed to use them.

pumpkin and pea risotto
with toasted pumpkin seeds
risotto alla zucca e piselli

1 stick unsalted butter

3 tablespoons pumpkin seeds

¼–½ teaspoon ground red pepper

about 1 quart hot Vegetable Broth (page 15) or Light Chicken Broth (page 16)

1 large onion, finely chopped

1 lb. fresh butternut squash or pumpkin, peeled and finely chopped (2½ cups)

1½ cups risotto rice

3 tablespoons chopped fresh mint

1½ cups frozen peas, cooked and drained

¾ cup freshly grated Parmesan cheese

sea salt and freshly ground black pepper

Serves 6

Put half the butter in a saucepan, melt until foaming, then add the pumpkin seeds. Stir over medium heat until the seeds begin to brown, then stir in the ground red pepper, salt, and pepper. Remove from the heat and keep the mixture warm.

Put the broth in a saucepan and keep at a gentle simmer. Melt the remaining butter in a large, heavy saucepan and add the onion. Cook gently for 10 minutes until soft, golden, and translucent but not browned. Add the squash or pumpkin, and cook, stirring constantly over the heat for 15 minutes until it begins to soften and disintegrate. Mash the pumpkin in the pan with a potato masher or fork. Stir in the rice to coat with the butter and mashed pumpkin. Cook for a couple of minutes to toast the grains.

Begin adding the broth, a large ladle at a time, stirring gently until each ladle has almost been absorbed by the rice. The risotto should be kept at a bare simmer throughout cooking, so don't let the rice dry out—add more broth as necessary. Continue until the rice is tender and creamy, but the grains still firm. (This should take 15–20 minutes depending on the type of rice used—check the package instructions.)

Taste, season well with salt and pepper, and stir in the mint, peas, and all the Parmesan. Cover and let rest for a couple of minutes so the risotto can relax, then serve immediately, sprinkled with the pumpkin seeds. You may like to add a little more hot broth to the risotto just before you serve to loosen it, but don't let it wait around too long or the rice will turn mushy.

A pretty, delicate risotto made even more special with sliced zucchini flowers (squash blossom). There are two types of flower—male and female. The females will produce a zucchini if fertilized, while the male flowers are the ones used for stuffing. They are just a flower on a stalk and the central spike must be removed before cooking. Squash blossom are sold in Italian produce stores and some farmers' markets.

squash blossom risotto
risotto con fiori di zucchine

about 6 cups hot Light Chicken Broth (page 16) or Vegetable Broth (page 15)

1 stick unsalted butter

1 onion, finely chopped

1 celery stalk, finely chopped

2 cups risotto rice

4 zucchini, grated

½ cup freshly grated Parmesan cheese

4–6 squash blossom, trimmed and finely sliced

sea salt and freshly ground black pepper

Serves 4

Put the broth in a saucepan and keep at a gentle simmer. Melt half the butter in a large, heavy saucepan and add the onion and celery. Cook gently for 10 minutes until soft, golden, and translucent but not browned. Add the rice and stir until well coated with the butter and heated through.

Begin adding the broth, a large ladle at a time, stirring gently until each ladle has almost been absorbed by the rice. The risotto should be kept at a bare simmer throughout cooking, so don't let the rice dry out—add more broth as necessary. Halfway through cooking, stir in the grated zucchini. Continue cooking and adding broth until the rice is tender and creamy, but the grains still firm. (This should take 15–20 minutes, depending on the type of rice used—check the package instructions.)

Taste, season well with salt and pepper, beat in the remaining butter and all the Parmesan, then stir in the squash blossom. Cover and let rest for a couple of minutes so the risotto can relax, then serve immediately. You may like to add a little more hot broth to the risotto just before you serve to loosen it, but don't let it wait around too long or the rice will turn mushy.

We make this risotto in our cooking classes in Tuscany in October, when fresh porcini mushrooms are around—and it's a great favorite. Any kind of fresh wild mushroom will make this taste wonderful, but it can be made very successfully using a mixture of cultivated mushrooms and reconstituted dried Italian porcini. In Italy, a wild herb called *nepitella* is often used when cooking wild mushrooms. It is a type of wild catnip and complements the mushrooms very well.

wild mushroom risotto

risotto ai funghi di bosco

6 cups hot Light Chicken Broth (page 16) or Vegetable Broth (page 15)

1 stick unsalted butter

1 large onion, finely chopped

2 garlic cloves, finely chopped

3 cups mixed wild mushrooms, cleaned and coarsely chopped (or a mixture of wild and fresh, or 1½ cups cultivated mushrooms, plus 1 oz. dried porcini soaked in warm water for 20 minutes, drained and chopped)

1 tablespoon chopped fresh thyme

1 tablespoon chopped fresh marjoram (or *nepitella*)

⅔ cup dry white wine or vermouth

2½ cups risotto rice

¾ cup freshly grated Parmesan cheese, plus extra to serve

sea salt and freshly ground black pepper

Serves 6

Put the broth in a saucepan and keep at a gentle simmer. Melt the butter in a large, heavy saucepan and add the onion and garlic. Cook gently for 10 minutes until soft, golden, and translucent but not browned. Stir in the mushrooms and herbs, then cook over medium heat for 3 minutes to heat through. Pour in the wine and boil hard until it has reduced and almost disappeared. This will remove the taste of raw alcohol. Stir in the rice and sauté with the onion and mushrooms until dry and slightly opaque.

Begin adding the broth, a large ladle at a time, stirring until each ladle has been absorbed by the rice. Continue until the rice is tender and creamy, but the grains still firm. (This should take about 15–20 minutes depending on the type of rice used—check the package instructions.)

Taste and season well with salt and pepper. Stir in the Parmesan, cover, let rest for a couple of minutes, then serve immediately with extra grated Parmesan.

When the Italian asparagus season is in full flush, it is celebrated with great gusto. Asparagus of all types is for sale, the most prized being the fat white asparagus. It is usually cooked further than *al dente*, which really brings out the flavor. This is about the only time I like to have shaved Parmesan on a risotto—the contrast of textures is wonderful.

asparagus risotto
with a poached egg and parmesan
risotto agli asparagi con uovo in camicia e parmigiano

1 lb. fresh green or purple-tipped asparagus

about 6 cups hot Vegetable Broth (page 15) or Light Chicken Broth (page 16)

1 teaspoon tarragon wine vinegar or white wine vinegar

6 fresh eggs, cracked into separate cups

1 stick unsalted butter

2 large shallots, finely chopped

2⅓ cups risotto rice, preferably carnaroli

½ cup freshly grated Parmesan cheese

sea salt and freshly ground black pepper

to serve

1 tablespoon chopped fresh parsley and tarragon, mixed

Parmesan shavings

Serves 6

Trim the base from each asparagus stem, but do no more than that. Put the broth in a wide saucepan and heat to simmering. Add the asparagus and boil for about 6 minutes until just tender. Drain, reserving the asparagus-flavored broth, and transferring it to a regular saucepan to simmer. Plunge the asparagus into a bowl of cold water to cool and set the color, then cut into small pieces. If the ends of the asparagus stalks are very tough, cut them off, cut in half lengthwise, and scrape out the insides and reserve. Add the tough parts to the broth. Reserve a few tips to serve.

To poach the eggs, fill a medium saucepan with cold water and bring to a boil. When the water is boiling, add the wine vinegar, then give it a good stir to create a whirlpool. Slip an egg into the vortex, then simmer very gently for 2–3 minutes. Using a slotted spoon, transfer the poached egg to a pan of warm water. Repeat the same procedure with the other eggs. Keep them warm while you make the risotto.

Melt half the butter in a large, heavy saucepan and add the shallots. Cook gently for 5–6 minutes until soft, golden, and translucent but not browned. Add the rice and asparagus scrapings to the shallots and stir until well coated with the butter and heated through. Begin adding the broth, a large ladle at a time (keeping back the asparagus trimmings), stirring gently until each ladle has almost been absorbed by the rice. The risotto should be kept at a bare simmer throughout cooking, so don't let the rice dry out—add more broth as necessary. Continue until the rice is tender and creamy, but the grains still firm. (This should take 15–20 minutes depending on the type of rice used—check the package instructions.)

Taste, season well with salt and pepper, and beat in the remaining butter and all the Parmesan. Fold in the drained asparagus. Cover, let rest for a few minutes so the risotto can relax and the asparagus heat through, then serve immediately. You may like to add a little more hot broth to the risotto just before you serve to loosen it, but don't let it wait around too long or the rice will turn mushy. Serve the risotto topped with a drained poached egg, sprinkled with parsley and tarragon and Parmesan shavings.

The secret of this risotto is not to cut the vegetables too big—they should be jewel-like in the rice. Sometimes, I stir half into the risotto and pile the rest on top. Sprinkle with basil and trickle good olive oil over the top before serving.

oven-roasted mediterranean vegetable risotto

risotto con verdure del mediterraneo

1 zucchini, trimmed and cut into 1-inch chunks

1 eggplant, trimmed and cut into 1-inch chunks

1 red bell pepper, halved, seeded, and cut into squares

1 carrot, cut into sticks

½ cup olive oil

about 6 cups hot Vegetable Broth (page 15)

7 tablespoons unsalted butter

1 red onion, finely chopped

2 garlic cloves, finely chopped

1 tablespoon freshly squeezed lemon juice

1 teaspoon crushed coriander seeds

a pinch of ground red pepper

2⅓ cups risotto rice

⅔ cup dry white wine

3 tablespoons finely sliced fresh basil

sea salt and freshly ground black pepper

to serve

basil leaves

freshly grated Parmesan cheese

extra virgin olive oil

Serves 6

Put the zucchini, eggplant, pepper, and carrot into a large roasting pan, pour over the oil and ½ cup water and toss well to coat. Roast in a preheated oven at 400°F for about 25 minutes, turning often until the vegetables are tender and caramelizing. Remove from the oven and tip into a colander set over a bowl. Reserve the cooking juices. Cool the vegetables.

Put the broth in a saucepan and keep at a gentle simmer. Melt half the butter in a large, heavy saucepan and add the onion, garlic, and the lemon juice. Cook gently for 10 minutes until soft, golden, and translucent but not browned. Add the coriander seeds and ground red pepper, then the rice, and stir until well coated with the butter and heated through. Pour in the reserved roasting juices and wine and boil hard until they have reduced and almost disappeared. This will remove the taste of raw alcohol.

Begin adding the broth, a large ladle at a time, stirring gently until each ladle has almost been absorbed by the rice. The risotto should be kept at a bare simmer throughout cooking, so don't let the rice dry out—add more broth as necessary. Continue until the rice is tender and creamy, but the grains still firm. (This should take 15–20 minutes depending on the type of rice used—check the package instructions.)

Taste and season well with salt and pepper, then beat in the remaining butter. Reserve a few spoonfuls of the vegetables, then fold in the remainder and the basil, cover, and let rest for a few minutes so the risotto can relax and the vegetables heat through. Serve immediately. You may like to add a little more hot broth to the risotto just before you serve to loosen it, but don't let it wait around too long or the rice will turn mushy.

Top with the basil, reserved vegetables, Parmesan, and a trickle of olive oil.

Smoky grilled artichokes are wonderful combined with nutty pecorino. Pecorino is made from ewes' milk (*latte de pecora*) and when aged can be grated like Parmesan. When young, it has a Cheddar-like texture and a rich, nutty flavor.

artichoke and pecorino risotto
risotto ai carciofi e pecorino

12 fresh artichokes, or 12 marinated artichokes, or 8 frozen artichoke hearts, thawed

about 6 cups hot Light Chicken Broth (page 16) or Vegetable Broth (page 15)

1 stick unsalted butter, plus extra for cooking (optional)

1 onion, finely chopped

2⅓ cups risotto rice

⅔ cup dry white wine

¾ cup freshly grated pecorino cheese

sea salt and freshly ground black pepper

Serves 4

First prepare the fresh artichokes, if using (see below), then brush with olive oil and cook for 5 minutes on a stove-top grill pan, turning often. If using thawed frozen ones, slice them and sauté in a little butter until golden.

Put the broth in a saucepan and keep at a gentle simmer. Melt half the butter in a large, heavy saucepan and add the onion. Cook gently for 10 minutes until soft, golden, and translucent but not browned. Add the rice and stir until well coated with the butter and heated through. Pour in the wine and boil hard until it has reduced and almost disappeared. This will remove the taste of raw alcohol.

Begin adding the broth, a large ladle at a time, stirring gently until each ladle has almost been absorbed by the rice. The risotto should be kept at a bare simmer throughout cooking, so don't let the rice dry out—add more broth as necessary. Continue until the rice is tender and creamy, but the grains still firm. (This should take 15–20 minutes depending on the type of rice used—check the package instructions.)

Taste and season well with salt and pepper, then beat in the remaining butter and all the pecorino. Fold in the artichokes. Cover and let rest for a couple of minutes so the risotto can relax, then serve immediately. You may like to add a little more hot broth to the risotto just before you serve to loosen it, but don't let it wait around too long or the rice will turn mushy.

Note To prepare fresh young artichokes, you will need 1 lemon, halved, and purple-green baby artichokes with stems and heads, about 4 inches long. Fill a large bowl with water and squeeze in the juice of ½ lemon to acidulate it. Use the other lemon half to rub the cut portions of the artichoke as you work. Trim the artichokes by snapping off the dark outer leaves, starting at the base. Trim the stalk down to about 2 inches. Trim away the dark green outer layer at the base and peel the fibrous outside of the stalk with a vegetable peeler. Cut about ½ inch off the tip of each artichoke heart. Put each artichoke in the lemony water until needed—this will stop them discoloring. Drain and use as required.

A wonderfully light and fragrant risotto, perfect for the summer to serve with cold chicken or fish. Try to use the more fragrant soft herbs here—the more the merrier.

green herb risotto
with white wine and lemon
risotto alle erbe verdi e limone

about 6 cups hot Vegetable Broth (page 15) or Light Chicken Broth (page 16)

1 stick unsalted butter

8 scallions, green and white parts, finely chopped

⅔ cup dry white wine

finely grated zest and juice of 1 large unwaxed lemon

2⅓ cups risotto rice

¼ cup chopped fresh herbs such as parsley, basil, marjoram, and thyme

¾ cup freshly grated Parmesan cheese

sea salt and freshly ground black pepper

Serves 4–6

Put the broth in a saucepan and keep at a gentle simmer. Melt half the butter in a large, heavy saucepan and add the scallions. Cook gently for 3–5 minutes until soft. Pour in the wine, add half the lemon zest, and boil hard until the wine has reduced and almost disappeared. This will remove the taste of raw alcohol. Add the rice and stir until well coated with butter and onions and heated through.

Begin adding the hot broth, a large ladle at a time, stirring until each ladle has been absorbed by the rice. Continue until the rice is tender and creamy, but the grains still firm. (This should take 15–20 minutes depending on the type of rice used—check the package instructions.)

Taste and season well with salt and lots of freshly ground black pepper. Stir in the remaining butter, the lemon zest, juice, herbs, and Parmesan. Cover and let rest for a couple of minutes, then serve immediately.

Carrots are an underestimated vegetable. When in their prime, they are sweet and juicy and roast perfectly. The watercress pesto, which looks spectacular with the orange risotto has a nutty, peppery taste. Arugula could be used instead of watercress with the same peppery result.

caramelized carrot risotto
with watercress pesto
risotto con carote arrostite e pesto al crescione

1 lb. carrots, cut into chunky rounds or batons (3½ cups)

¼ cup olive oil

sea salt and freshly ground black pepper

watercress pesto

2 handfuls of watercress leaves, without stalks

1 garlic clove, chopped

3 tablespoons freshly grated Parmesan cheese

¼ cup shelled hazelnuts

⅓ cup extra virgin olive oil, plus extra for covering

sea salt and freshly ground black pepper

risotto

about 6 cups hot Vegetable Broth (page 15) or Light Chicken Broth (page 16)

1 stick unsalted butter

1 onion, finely chopped

2 cups risotto rice

⅔ cup dry white wine

¾ cup freshly grated Parmesan cheese

sea salt and freshly ground black pepper

Serves 4

Toss the carrots in the olive oil, spread in a roasting pan, and sprinkle with salt and pepper. Roast in a preheated oven at 400°F for 20 minutes, turning occasionally until they begin to caramelize.

Meanwhile, to make the pesto, put the watercress, garlic, Parmesan, hazelnuts, olive oil, salt, and pepper in a food processor and blend until smooth, scraping down any bits that cling to the side of the bowl. Alternatively, pound with a mortar and pestle. Cover with a thin layer of oil and set aside.

To make the risotto, put the broth in a saucepan and keep at a gentle simmer. Melt half the butter in a large, heavy saucepan and add the onion. Cook gently for 10 minutes until soft, golden, and translucent but not browned. Add the rice and stir until well coated with the butter and heated through. Pour in the wine and boil hard until it has reduced and almost disappeared. This will remove the taste of raw alcohol.

Begin adding the broth, a large ladle at a time, stirring gently until each ladle has almost been absorbed by the rice. The risotto should be kept at a bare simmer throughout cooking, so don't let the rice dry out—add more broth as necessary. Continue until the rice is tender and creamy, but the grains still firm. (This should take 15–20 minutes depending on the type of rice used—check the package instructions.) Stir in the carrots and pan juices. Add salt and pepper to taste and beat in the remaining butter and half the Parmesan.

Cover and let rest for a few minutes so the risotto can relax and the cheese melt, then serve immediately. You may like to add a little more hot broth to the risotto just before you serve to loosen it, but don't let it wait around too long or the rice will turn mushy. Serve in warm bowls with a spoon of pesto on top and sprinkled with the remaining Parmesan.

A delicate fennel and lemon risotto with the taste of the Mediterranean stirred in just before serving. I like the rich earthiness of shiny, oven-dried black olives, but if you prefer something less pungent, use large, juicy green olives instead.

fennel and black olive risotto

risotto ai finocchi con olive nere

fennel and black olive relish

⅓ cup extra virgin olive oil

1 onion, finely chopped

1 garlic clove, crushed

1 fennel bulb, trimmed and chopped

5 sun-dried tomatoes in oil, drained and coarsely chopped

1¼ cups Greek-style (dry-cured) olives, pitted

1 fresh bay leaf

12 basil leaves, torn

2 tablespoons aniseed liqueur, such as Sambuca

sea salt and freshly ground black pepper

fennel risotto

about 1 quart hot Vegetable Broth (page 15) or Light Chicken Broth (page 16)

1 stick unsalted butter

1 onion, finely chopped

3 fennel bulbs, trimmed and finely chopped (green tops included)

finely grated zest of 1 unwaxed lemon

1½ cups risotto rice

⅔ cup dry white wine

freshly grated Parmesan cheese, to serve

Serves 6

To make the relish, heat 2 tablespoons of the olive oil in a medium saucepan and gently cook the onion, garlic, and fennel for a few minutes until softening. Add the sun-dried tomatoes, olives and bay leaf and continue to cook for 2–3 minutes more. Season to taste with salt and pepper, remove the bay leaf, then stir in the basil. Transfer to a food processor and blend to a coarse texture. Stir in the aniseed liqueur and remaining olive oil. Cover and set aside.

To make the risotto, put the broth in a saucepan and keep at a gentle simmer. Melt half the butter in a large, heavy saucepan and add the onion. Cook gently for 5 minutes until soft, golden and translucent, but not browned. Stir in the fennel and lemon zest and continue to cook for 10 minutes until softening. Add the rice and stir until well coated with the butter and heated through. Pour in the wine and boil hard until it has reduced and almost disappeared. This will remove the taste of raw alcohol.

Begin adding the broth, a large ladle at a time, stirring gently until each ladle has almost been absorbed by the rice. The risotto should be kept at a bare simmer throughout cooking, so don't let the rice dry out—add more broth as necessary. Continue until the rice is tender and creamy, but the grains still firm and the fennel absolutely tender. (This should take 15–20 minutes depending on the type of rice used—check the package instructions.)

Taste and season well with salt and pepper, then beat in the remaining butter. Cover and let rest for a couple of minutes so the risotto can relax, then serve immediately. Just before serving, you may like to add a little more hot broth to loosen the risotto, but don't let it wait around too long or the rice will turn mushy. Top with the fennel and black olive relish before serving with extra grated Parmesan.

A lovely soup to serve in the summer when fresh peas are in abundance. Vialone nano is the favorite rice for risotto in the Veneto region. It is a *semifino* short-grain rice, best for soup and risotto, but arborio, a *superfino* used mainly for risotto, will do very nicely. This has very ancient roots, and was flavored with fennel seeds at one time. Parsley is the usual addition, but I prefer mint in the summer.

venetian pea and rice thick soup
risi e bisi

2 lb. fresh peas in the pod or 3 cups frozen peas

5 cups hot Light Chicken Broth (page 16), Beef or Veal Broth (page 19), or Vegetable Broth (page 15)

2 tablespoons olive oil

4½ tablespoons unsalted butter

3 tablespoons finely chopped pancetta or prosciutto

the white parts of 4 scallions, finely chopped

1 cup risotto rice, preferably vialone nano

3 tablespoons chopped fresh parsley or mint

freshly grated Parmesan cheese

sea salt and freshly ground black pepper

Serves 4

Shell the peas and set aside. Slowly bring the broth to a boil with the pea pods (if using) while you prepare the pancetta and onion base.

Heat the olive oil with half the butter and, when melted, add the pancetta and onion. Cook for about 5 minutes but do not let it brown. Add the rice, stir for a few minutes to toast it, then add the hot broth. Simmer for 10 minutes, stirring from time to time. Add the peas, cook for another 5–7 minutes, and stir in the remaining butter, parsley or mint, and Parmesan.

Taste and season with salt and pepper, then serve immediately. The rice grains should not be too mushy, and the soup should be thick and soupy, but not at all heavy. Add more broth or water if necessary to thin it down.

The charm of this risotto is found in the delicate flavors and colors of spring. The vegetables are small and sweet, the herbs fresh and fragrant. Don't be tempted to skimp on the herbs here—as well as imparting intense flavor to the risotto, they add a beautiful touch of spring green. Sometimes I blend them with the remaining butter (melted) to give a bright green liquid to beat in at the end.

spring risotto with herbs
risotto primavera alle erbe

about 6 cups hot Light Chicken Broth (page 16) or Vegetable Broth (page 15)

1 stick unsalted butter

6 scallions, finely chopped

2 garlic cloves, finely chopped, crushed

1¼ cups cubed carrots or a bunch of tiny new carrots, trimmed and scraped but kept whole

2 cups risotto rice, preferably carnaroli

4 oz. asparagus spears, trimmed and cut into 1-inch lengths

¾ cup thin green beans, cut into 1-inch lengths

⅓ cup fresh or frozen peas or fava beans, thawed if frozen

⅓ cup chopped mixed fresh herbs, such as chives, dill, flat-leaf parsley, mint, chervil, and tarragon

½ cup freshly grated Parmesan cheese, plus extra to serve

sea salt and freshly ground black pepper

Serves 4

Put the broth in a saucepan and keep at a gentle simmer. Melt half the butter in a large, heavy saucepan and add the scallions, garlic, and carrots. Cook gently for 5 minutes until the scallions are soft and translucent but not browned. Add the rice and stir until well coated with the butter and heated through.

Begin adding the broth, a large ladle at a time, stirring gently until each ladle has almost been absorbed by the rice. The risotto should be kept at a bare simmer throughout cooking, so don't let the rice dry out—add more broth as necessary. After 10 minutes, add the asparagus, beans, and peas and continue until the vegetables are tender and the rice is tender and creamy, but the grains still firm. (This should take 15–20 minutes depending on the type of rice used—check the package instructions.)

Taste and season well with salt and pepper, then stir in the remaining butter, the herbs, and the Parmesan. Cover and let rest for a couple of minutes so the risotto can relax, then serve immediately with extra freshly grated Parmesan cheese. You may like to add a little more hot broth to the risotto just before you serve to loosen it, but don't let it wait around too long or the rice will turn mushy.

A dish from the Veneto, where vialone nano rice is grown, as well as several varieties of radicchio. Stirring in a good spoonful of mascarpone or cream at the end enriches the risotto and adds sweetness. The risotto has both a sweet and a bitter flavor. I like to add a few currants plumped up for 20 minutes in warm grappa for an added surprise.

creamy radicchio and mascarpone risotto

risotto cremoso al radicchio e mascarpone

about 6 cups hot Light Chicken Broth (page 16) or Vegetable Broth (page 15)

1 stick unsalted butter

2 carrots, finely diced

½ cup smoked pancetta or prosciutto, finely cubed

2 garlic cloves, finely chopped

1 lb. radicchio, finely shredded

2⅓ cups risotto rice

sea salt and freshly ground black pepper

2 tablespoons currants soaked in ¼ cup warm grappa for 20 minutes (optional)

3 tablespoons mascarpone cheese or heavy cream

¾ cup freshly grated Parmesan cheese

Serves 6

Put the broth in a saucepan and keep at a gentle simmer. Melt half the butter in a large, heavy saucepan and add the carrots. Cook gently for 5 minutes until softening, then add the pancetta and garlic, and cook for 4 minutes until just beginning to brown. Stir in the radicchio and cook for 5 minutes until it begins to wilt. Add the rice and stir until heated through. Add a ladle of hot broth and simmer, stirring until absorbed. Continue adding the broth ladle by ladle, making sure the rice is never dry, until all the broth is absorbed. The rice should be tender and creamy but still have some bite to it (15–20 minutes depending on the type of rice used—check the package instructions).

Taste and season well with salt and plenty of pepper. Add the soaked currants, if using, and stir in the remaining butter, the mascarpone or cream, and the Parmesan. Cover and let rest for a couple of minutes, then serve immediately.

An amazing risotto to serve on its own as a first course or to accompany meat or game dishes. This risotto needs the sweetness of the vegetables to balance the acidity from the wine. Use a good wine that you would not be ashamed to drink, and you will achieve perfect results. Use a cheap, undrinkable wine and the risotto will be inedible. Brighten it up with a scattering of emerald green chopped parsley.

red wine risotto
risotto al barolo

about 6 cups hot Vegetable Broth (page 15) or Light Chicken Broth (page 16)

1 stick unsalted butter

1 small red onion, finely chopped

1 small carrot, finely chopped

1 small celery stalk, finely chopped

3 tablespoons pancetta or prosciutto, finely chopped (optional)

2½ cups risotto rice

1¼ cups full-bodied red wine, such as Barolo

1¼ cups freshly grated Parmesan cheese

sea salt and freshly ground black pepper

chopped fresh parsley, to serve

Serves 4–6

Put the broth in a saucepan and keep at a gentle simmer. Melt half the butter in a large, heavy saucepan and add the onion, carrot, and celery. Cook gently for 10 minutes until soft, golden, and translucent but not browned. Add the pancetta (if using) and cook for another 2 minutes. Add the rice and stir until well coated with the butter and heated through. Pour in the wine and boil hard until it has been reduced by half. This will remove the taste of raw alcohol.

Begin adding the broth, a large ladle at a time, stirring gently until each ladle has almost been absorbed by the rice. The risotto should be kept at a bare simmer throughout cooking, so don't let the rice dry out—add more broth as necessary. Continue until the rice is tender and creamy, but the grains still firm. (This should take 15–20 minutes depending on the type of rice used—check the package instructions.)

Taste and season well with salt and pepper, then beat in the remaining butter and all the Parmesan. Cover and let rest for a couple of minutes so the risotto can relax, then serve immediately. You may like to add a little more hot broth to the risotto just before you serve to loosen it, but don't let it wait around too long or the rice will turn mushy. Serve sprinkled with parsley.

cheese and eggs

When you have nothing except risotto rice in the pantry, and a chunk of Parmesan and some butter in the refrigerator, yet feel the need for comfort and luxury, this is the risotto for you. It is pale, golden, smooth, and creamy and relies totally on the quality of the rice, butter, and cheese. I would use real Parmigiano Reggiano, with its sweet, nutty flavor, and nothing else.

parmesan and butter risotto
risotto alla parmigiana

about 6 cups hot Light Chicken Broth (page 16) or Vegetable Broth (page 15)

1 stick plus 3 tablespoons unsalted butter

1 onion, finely chopped

2½ cups risotto rice, preferably carnaroli

⅔ cup dry white wine

1 cup freshly grated Parmesan cheese

sea salt and freshly ground black pepper

Serves 4–6

Put the broth in a saucepan and keep at a gentle simmer. Melt half the butter in a large, heavy saucepan and add the onion. Cook gently for 10 minutes until soft, golden, and translucent but not browned. Add the rice and stir until well coated with the butter and heated through. Pour in the wine and boil hard until it has reduced and almost disappeared. This will remove any raw alcohol taste.

Begin adding the broth, a large ladle at a time, stirring gently until each ladle has almost been absorbed by the rice. The risotto should be kept at a bare simmer throughout cooking, so don't let the rice dry out—add more broth as necessary. Continue until the rice is tender and creamy, but the grains still firm. (This should take 15–20 minutes depending on the type of rice used— check the package instructions.)

Taste and season well with salt and pepper, then stir in the remaining butter and all the Parmesan. Cover and let rest for a couple of minutes so the risotto can relax and the cheese melt, then serve immediately. You may like to add a little more broth just before you serve, but don't let the risotto wait around too long or the rice will turn mushy.

This is not to be confused with *risotto alla milanese,* which accompanies the famous dish *osso buco,* enriched with delicious beef bone marrow. However, this recipe does the job very nicely, producing a rich, creamy risotto with the delicate taste of saffron. Saffron powder can also be used, but make sure it is real saffron and not just ground stamens of the safflower. Saffron will always be relatively expensive when bought outside its country of origin, and is a great thing to take home with you if you are visiting Italy or Spain, where it can be found at a good price.

saffron risotto
risotto allo zafferano

about 6 cups hot Light Chicken Broth (page 16)
or Vegetable Broth (page 15)

1 stick unsalted butter

1 onion, finely chopped

2⅓ cups risotto rice

⅔ cup dry white wine

16 saffron threads or ½ teaspoon ground saffron

¾ cup freshly grated Parmesan cheese

sea salt and freshly ground black pepper

Serves 4–6

Put the broth in a saucepan and keep at a gentle simmer. Melt half the butter in a large, heavy saucepan and add the onion. Cook gently for 10 minutes until soft, golden, and translucent but not browned. Add the rice and stir until well coated with the butter and heated through. Pour in the wine and boil hard until it has reduced and almost disappeared. This will remove any raw alcohol taste.

Begin adding the broth, a large ladle at a time, adding the saffron after the first ladle. Stir gently until each ladle has almost been absorbed by the rice. The risotto should be kept at a bare simmer throughout cooking, so don't let the rice dry out—add more broth as necessary. Continue until the rice is tender and creamy, but the grains still firm. (This should take 15–20 minutes depending on the type of rice used—check the package instructions.)

Taste and season well with salt and pepper, then stir in the remaining butter and all the Parmesan. Cover and let rest for a couple of minutes so the risotto can relax, then serve immediately. You may like to add a little more broth just before serving to loosen it, but don't let the risotto wait around too long or the rice will turn mushy.

When you dip your fork into this risotto, you will come across pockets of melting mozzarella. Mix in the tomato topping and you will make more strings. Try to use *mozzarella di bufala*–it has a fresh, lactic bite well-suited to this recipe.

mozzarella and sunblushed tomato risotto with basil
risotto con mozzarella e pomodori semi-secchi

about 6 cups hot Light Chicken Broth (page 16) or Vegetable Broth (page 15)

1 stick unsalted butter

1 onion, finely chopped

2 cups risotto rice

⅔ cup dry white wine

8 oz. mozzarella cheese balls, cut into ½-inch cubes

¼ cup chopped fresh basil

10 oz. sun-blushed tomatoes•

sea salt and freshly ground black pepper

to serve

extra basil leaves

freshly grated Parmesan cheese

Serves 4

*If you are unable to find sun-blushed tomatoes, buy 1 lb. organic grape tomatoes and semi-dry them in a preheated oven at 250°F for about 1 hour.

Put the broth in a saucepan and keep at a gentle simmer. Melt half the butter in a large, heavy saucepan and add the onion. Cook gently for 10 minutes until soft, golden, and translucent but not browned. Add the rice and stir until well coated with the butter and heated through. Pour in the wine and boil hard until it has reduced and almost disappeared. This will remove the taste of raw alcohol.

Begin adding the broth, a large ladle at a time, stirring gently until each ladle has almost been absorbed by the rice. The risotto should be kept at a bare simmer throughout cooking, so don't let the rice dry out—add more broth as necessary. Continue until the rice is tender and creamy, but the grains still firm. (This should take 15–20 minutes depending on the type of rice used—check the package instructions.)

Taste and season well with salt and pepper, then beat in the remaining butter. You may like to add a little more hot broth at this stage to loosen the risotto. Fold in the cubed mozzarella and chopped basil. Cover and let rest for a couple of minutes so the risotto can relax and the cheese melt. Carefully ladle into warm bowls and put a pile of tomatoes in the center of each one. Top with basil leaves and serve immediately with a bowl of grated Parmesan.

Gorgonzola is a strong cheese with blue-green marbling. The mold is injected into the cheese and left in temperature-controlled store rooms or caves. Factory-made cheese tends to be firmer, with a regular crazing of blue-green. Artisan or farm-made Gorgonzola, left in caves to develop the injected mold naturally, produces a creamy, less densely marbled cheese. In Italy, you buy Gorgonzola either *dolce* or *piccante*—mild or strong. I like *piccante*. Dolcelatte is made for the export market.

gorgonzola and ricotta risotto
with crisp sage leaves
risotto al gorgonzola, ricotta e salvia

about 6 cups hot Light Chicken Broth (page 16) or Vegetable Broth (page 15)

1 stick unsalted butter

1 onion, finely chopped

2 cups risotto rice

⅓ cup dry white vermouth

1 tablespoon chopped fresh sage leaves

¾ cup Gorgonzola cheese, crumbled

¾ cup fresh ricotta cheese

sea salt and freshly ground black pepper

crisp sage leaves

about 30 sage leaves with stalks

sea salt

oil, for deep-frying

electric deep-fryer or wok

Serves 4

To make the crisp sage leaves, pat them thoroughly dry. Heat the oil to 350°F in a deep-fryer or wok. If using a fryer, put the leaves in the basket and lower into the hot oil. It will hiss alarmingly, but don't worry. Immediately the hissing has stopped, lift the basket out and shake off the excess oil. (If using a wok, use tongs or a slotted spoon.) Spread the leaves on paper towels to drain. Season with a sprinkling of salt and set aside. They will crisp up as they cool.

Put the broth in a saucepan and keep at a gentle simmer. Melt half the butter in a large, heavy saucepan and add the onion. Cook gently for 10 minutes until soft, golden, and translucent but not browned. Add the rice and stir until well coated with the butter and heated through. Pour in the vermouth and boil hard until it has reduced and almost disappeared. This will remove the taste of raw alcohol. Stir in the chopped fresh sage.

Begin adding the broth, a large ladle at a time, stirring gently until each ladle has almost been absorbed by the rice. The risotto should be kept at a bare simmer throughout cooking, so don't let the rice dry out—add more broth as necessary. About halfway through the cooking time, stir in the Gorgonzola until melted. Continue adding broth and cooking until the rice is tender and creamy, but the grains still firm. (This should take 15–20 minutes depending on the type of rice used—check the package instructions.) The risotto should be quite loose, but not soupy.

Taste and season well with salt and pepper, then beat in the ricotta and remaining butter. Cover and let rest for a couple of minutes so the risotto can relax. You may like to add a little more hot broth to the risotto just before you serve to loosen it, but don't let it wait around too long or the rice will turn mushy. Serve with the fried sage leaves on top.

A risotto made with meltingly soft Fontina cheese or even raclette becomes almost a fondue. Bresaola is often served as a side dish with raclette and fondue, and makes a delicious topping to the risotto. Produced around Valtellina in Lombardy, bresaola is raw fillet of beef, salted then air-dried. It is always sliced very thinly and is a beautiful, deep garnet-red color.

raclette or fontina risotto
with bresaola

risotto alla raclette o fontina con bresaola

about 6 cups hot Vegetable Broth (page 15) or Light Chicken Broth (page 16)

1 stick unsalted butter

1 onion, finely chopped

2⅓ cups risotto rice

⅔ cup fruity white wine

4 oz. Fontina or raclette cheese, rinds removed and remainder grated or chopped, about ¾ cup

6–8 thin slices bresaola, finely chopped, plus 8–12 thin slices extra, to serve

sea salt and freshly ground black pepper

Serves 4–6

Put the broth in a saucepan and keep at a gentle simmer. Melt half the butter in a large, heavy saucepan and add the onion. Cook gently for 10 minutes until soft, golden, and translucent but not browned. Add the rice and stir until well coated with the butter and heated through. Pour in the wine and boil hard until it has reduced and almost disappeared. This will remove the taste of raw alcohol.

Begin adding the broth, a large ladle at a time, stirring gently until each ladle has almost been absorbed by the rice. The risotto should be kept at a bare simmer throughout cooking, so don't let the rice dry out—add more broth as necessary. Halfway through cooking, stir in the cheese until melted. Continue adding broth and cooking until the rice is tender and creamy, but the grains still firm. (This should take 15–20 minutes depending on the type of rice used—check the package instructions.)

Taste and season well with salt and pepper, then beat in the remaining butter and chopped bresaola. Cover and let rest for a couple of minutes so the risotto can relax. You may like to add a little more hot broth to the risotto just before you serve to loosen it, but don't let it wait around too long or the rice will turn mushy. The risotto should be quite loose. Serve with the remaining bresaola crumpled or draped on top.

Roasting a big batch of garlic makes sure that you will always have some in the refrigerator for adding to soups or even spreading on toast or bruschetta. I use two kinds of cheese here. The soft cheese melts creamily into the risotto, whereas the cheese with rind (*Bûcheron chèvre*) cut from a thick log, broils to perfection without collapsing—as long as it isn't too ripe.

roasted garlic risotto
with goat cheese and rosemary
risotto con caprino, aglio dorato e rosmarino

20 large garlic cloves, peeled (you will only use 8, but you can keep the rest in a jar of oil in the refrigerator)

⅓ cup extra virgin olive oil, plus extra for basting

4–6 large thick slices goat cheese with rind

4–6 small sprigs of rosemary, plus extra to serve

about 6 cups hot Light Chicken Broth (page 16)

1 red onion, finely chopped

2 tablespoons chopped fresh rosemary

2⅓ cups risotto rice

8 oz. soft mild goat cheese (the one with no rind)

½ cup freshly grated Parmesan cheese

sea salt and freshly ground black pepper

12-inch square of aluminum foil

a baking sheet

nonstick parchment paper

Serves 4–6

Put the garlic, 2 tablespoons of oil, salt, and pepper in a mixing bowl and toss well. Put the garlic in the middle of the foil, fold up the long ends, and fold together at the top to create a seal. Fold in the short ends to create a sealed package. Set on a baking sheet and roast in a preheated oven at 350°F for 20 minutes, then turn over, cut a small steam hole in the top (former underside), and roast the package upside down for a further 10 minutes. (This will keep wrapped tightly in the refrigerator for up to 1 week.) Reserve 8 cloves to use.

Put the sliced goat cheese on a broiler pan lined with the parchment. Brush with olive oil and put a rosemary sprig on each one. Sprinkle with pepper and set aside. Preheat the broiler.

Put the broth in a saucepan and keep at a gentle simmer. Heat the remaining olive oil in a heavy saucepan. Add the onion and cook gently for 5 minutes, then add the roasted garlic and half the chopped rosemary. Cook for a further 5 minutes, then stir in the rice until well coated with oil and heated through.

Begin adding the broth, a large ladle at a time, stirring gently until each ladle has almost been absorbed by the rice. The risotto should be kept at a bare simmer throughout cooking, so don't let the rice dry out—add more broth as necessary. Halfway through cooking the risotto, broil the sliced goats' cheese until browned on top. Continue until the rice is tender and creamy, but the grains still firm. (This should take 15–20 minutes depending on the type of rice used—check the package instructions.) Stir in the soft cheese and remaining rosemary.

Taste and season well with salt and pepper, then beat in the Parmesan cheese. Cover and let rest for a couple of minutes so the risotto can relax, then serve immediately in warm bowls. You may like to add a little more hot broth to the risotto just before you serve to loosen it, but don't let it wait around too long or the rice will turn mushy. Using a spatula, set a slice of broiled goat cheese on each serving and top with a sprig of rosemary.

This is a way of enjoying the taste of truffles without the enormous expense. Fresh white truffles from Alba are heaven shaved over a white risotto, but there are lots of products flavored with truffles. There's truffle butter, truffle oil (make sure it is the real thing and not just flavored with a chemical), and truffle paste or sauce. All these can be mixed with egg yolks, then added to the risotto as long as you don't add too much—it can be very overpowering. Parsley brings the whole thing alive and the best parsley in Italy is said to come from Lombardy.

truffled egg risotto

risotto all'uovo e tartufi

4 hard-cooked eggs

4 teaspoons truffle and porcini mushroom sauce or paste *(la truffata)*

about 6 cups hot Vegetable Broth (page 15) or Light Chicken Broth (page 16)

1 stick unsalted butter

1 onion, finely chopped

2 cups risotto rice

2–3 tablespoons chopped fresh flat leaf parsley

sea salt and freshly ground black pepper

parsley leaves, to serve

Serves 4

Cut the eggs in half and take out the yolks. Finely chop the whites. Mash the yolks in a small bowl with the truffle and mushroom sauce or paste.

Put the broth in a saucepan and keep at a gentle simmer. Melt half the butter in a large, heavy saucepan and add the onion. Cook gently for 10 minutes until soft, golden, and translucent but not browned. Add the rice and stir until well coated with the butter and heated through.

Begin adding the broth, a large ladle at a time, stirring gently until each ladle has almost been absorbed by the rice. The risotto should be kept at a bare simmer throughout cooking, so don't let the rice dry out—add more broth as necessary. Continue until the rice is tender and creamy, but the grains still firm. (This should take 15–20 minutes depending on the type of rice used—check the package instructions.)

Taste and season well with salt and pepper, then beat in the remaining butter, truffled egg yolks, chopped egg whites, and chopped parsley. Cover and let rest for a couple of minutes so the risotto can relax, then serve immediately. You may like to add a little more hot broth to the risotto just before you serve to loosen it, but don't let it wait around too long or the rice will turn mushy. Serve topped with the parsley leaves.

poultry and game

I couldn't resist this one—although it really is a French dish, it works so well with risotto. Confit chicken can be bought in cans if you can't be bothered to make it, but making your own is very satisfying and really incredibly easy. The duck fat or oil can be used over and over again if properly strained between each batch. Confit chicken is meltingly tender, and doesn't absorb fat or too much salt.

chicken confit risotto
risotto al pollo conservato

about 6 cups hot Light Chicken Broth (page 16)

1 stick unsalted butter
or ½ cup rendered duck fat (listed below)
or olive oil

1 onion, finely chopped

3 garlic cloves, finely chopped

1 carrot, finely chopped

1 celery stalk, finely chopped

2⅓ cups risotto rice

½ cup freshly grated Parmesan cheese

sea salt and freshly ground black pepper

chicken confit

4 chicken legs (thigh and drumstick joined)
with skin on

3 garlic cloves, finely chopped

2 teaspoons chopped fresh thyme

2 bay leaves

about 2¾ cups olive oil or 1 lb. duck fat

Serves 4

To make the chicken confit, start the day before. Put the chicken legs in a non-reactive dish and rub with 3 tablespoons of the salt, the garlic, and thyme. Turn the legs skin side up and tuck in the bay leaves. Cover the dish with plastic wrap and keep in the refrigerator overnight.

Remove the chicken from the refrigerator, rub off the excess salt, and rinse under running water. Pat the legs dry with paper towels. Closely pack them in a single layer in a baking dish and cover with warmed olive oil or melted duck fat, making sure the legs are completely covered by the oil or fat. Cook in a preheated oven at 350°F for about 45 minutes until cooked through. Set aside to cool completely in the oil or fat, then cover and refrigerate until needed. When ready to use, lift the chicken out of the oil or fat and wipe clean. Pull off the skin and take the meat from the bones and coarsely cut it up. Set aside.

Put the broth in a saucepan and keep at a gentle simmer. Melt half the butter in a large, heavy saucepan and add the onion, garlic, carrot, and celery. Cook gently for 10 minutes until soft, golden, and translucent but not browned. Add the rice and stir until well coated with the butter and heated through.

Begin adding the broth, a large ladle at a time, stirring gently until each ladle has almost been absorbed by the rice. The risotto should be kept at a bare simmer throughout cooking, so don't let the rice dry out—add more broth as necessary. Continue until the rice is tender and creamy, but the grains still firm. (This should take 15–20 minutes depending on the type of rice used—check the package instructions.)

Taste and season well with salt and pepper, then beat in the remaining butter and the Parmesan. Stir in the chicken and thyme. Cover and let rest for a couple of minutes so the risotto can relax and the chicken heat through, then serve immediately. You may like to add a little more hot broth to the risotto just before you serve to loosen it, but don't let it wait around too long or the rice will turn mushy.

My favorite cultivated mushrooms are the large, flat, open, almost black portobellos. They have much more flavor than younger ones with closed caps, and are almost the next best thing to wild mushrooms. They absorb a lot of butter and I like to get them really quite brown to concentrate the flavor. Tarragon goes particularly well with this combination, but can be overpowering, so don't use too much.

chicken and mushroom risotto
with tarragon
risotto al pollo, funghi e dragoncello

8 oz. large portobello mushrooms

1 stick plus 3 tablespoons unsalted butter

1 garlic clove, finely chopped

about 6 cups hot Light Chicken Broth (page 16)

1 onion, finely chopped

1 celery stalk, finely chopped

1¼ lb. boneless, skinless chicken thighs and breast, chopped finely

2⅓ cups risotto rice

1¼ cups dry white wine

2 teaspoons chopped fresh tarragon

¾ cup freshly grated Parmesan cheese

sea salt and freshly ground black pepper

chopped fresh parsley, to serve

Serves 6

To prepare the mushrooms, cut them into long slices. Melt 6 tablespoons of the butter in a skillet, add the mushrooms and garlic, and sauté over medium heat until browning at the edges. Transfer to a plate and set aside.

Put the broth in a saucepan and keep at a gentle simmer. Melt 2 tablespoons of the remaining butter in a large, heavy saucepan and add the onion and celery. Cook gently for 10 minutes until soft and golden but not browned. Add the chicken and cook for another 5 minutes, but do not let it color and harden. Stir in the rice until well coated with butter, heated through and beginning to smell "toasted." Pour in the wine, bring to a boil, and boil hard to reduce by half—this will concentrate the flavor and remove the raw taste of alcohol.

Begin adding the broth, a large ladle at a time, stirring gently until each ladle has been absorbed by the rice. The rice should always be at a gentle simmer. Continue in this way until the rice is tender and creamy, but the grains still firm. (This should take 15–20 minutes depending on the type of rice used—check the package instructions.)

Taste and season well with salt and pepper, then stir in the remaining butter, the tarragon and Parmesan. Cover and let rest for a couple of minutes to let the risotto relax. Reheat the mushrooms, then serve the risotto with the mushrooms piled on top, sprinkled with chopped parsley.

I first discovered the marriage of a little Vin Santo and chicken livers in Tuscany, when I was cooking a traditional topping of chicken livers for crostini. There wasn't an open bottle of wine handy, so I used a drop of Vin Santo. It was sublime. The sweet grapiness was perfect with chicken livers. Find the freshest, plumpest livers for this risotto.

chicken liver risotto
with vin santo

risotto ai fegatini e vin santo

6 oz. plump fresh chicken livers

about 6 cups hot Light Chicken Broth (page 16)
or Vegetable Broth (page 15)

1 stick unsalted butter

2 shallots, finely chopped

1 celery stalk, finely chopped

1 small carrot, finely chopped

3 tablespoons Italian Vin Santo or dry sherry

1 tablespoon sun-dried tomato paste or purée

2 cups risotto rice, preferably vialone nano

2 tablespoons salted capers, rinsed and chopped

3 tablespoons chopped fresh parsley

sea salt and freshly ground black pepper

Serves 4

Trim any stringy bits from the livers with a sharp knife. Cut away any discolored bits and cut into large (1-inch) pieces. Set aside.

Put the broth in a saucepan and keep at a gentle simmer. Melt half the butter in a large, heavy saucepan and add the shallots, celery, and carrot. Cook gently for 6–8 minutes until soft, golden, and translucent but not browned. Stir in the livers, then raise the heat until they are cooked and firm on the outside, soft and pink inside. Stir in the Vin Santo and tomato paste and boil hard until the liquid has all but evaporated. Add the rice and stir until well coated with the butter and vegetables and heated through.

Begin adding the broth, a large ladle at a time, stirring gently so as not to break up the chicken livers too much, until each ladle has almost been absorbed by the rice. The risotto should be kept at a bare simmer throughout cooking, so don't let the rice dry out—add more broth as necessary. Continue until the rice is tender and creamy, but the grains still firm (15–20 minutes depending on the type of rice used—check the package instructions).

Taste and season well with salt and pepper, then beat in the remaining butter, the capers, and parsley. Cover and let rest for a couple of minutes so the risotto can relax, then serve immediately. You may like to add a little more hot broth to the risotto just before you serve to loosen it, but don't let it wait around too long or the rice will turn mushy.

Make this risotto really soupy, with vialone nano rice, as served in the Veneto—the land of lagoons and wildfowl. Wild duck would make all the difference to this dish if you have access to it, giving it a rich, gamey taste. The anchovies are barely perceptible in the risotto, but they add a deep, savory flavor, which will make even the most domestic of ducks taste like game birds. The balsamic vinegar is my secret ingredient, again to give depth to the finished dish.

duck risotto with wilted spinach
risotto all'anatra con spinaci

about 6 cups hot Game Broth made with duck bones or Light Chicken Broth (page 16)

3 duck breasts with fat

1 stick unsalted butter or the skin from the duck breasts

1 onion, finely chopped

2 garlic cloves, finely chopped

½ cup chopped pancetta or prosciutto

1 tablespoon chopped fresh sage

1 tablespoon chopped fresh rosemary

finely grated zest and juice of 1 unwaxed lemon

4 anchovies, rinsed and chopped

⅔ cup dry white wine (optional)

2 tablespoons balsamic vinegar

2 cups risotto rice, such as vialone nano

2 cups firmly packed fresh spinach, washed

sea salt and freshly ground black pepper

¼ cup freshly grated Parmesan cheese, to serve

Serves 4

Put the broth in a saucepan and keep at a gentle simmer. Pull the fat off the duck breasts and chop it. Chop the duck meat into small pieces. Melt half the butter (or use the duck fat and skin and slowly sauté it in the pan for 5–10 minutes until it releases the fat, then remove the solids) in a large, heavy saucepan and add the onion and garlic. Cook for 10 minutes over medium heat until soft and beginning to caramelize.

Add the duck, pancetta, sage, rosemary, lemon zest, and anchovies and cook for 2–3 minutes until changing color, but not browning. Pour in the wine and balsamic vinegar and boil hard for 1 minute to boil off the alcohol. Add 2 ladles of broth, cover, and simmer very gently for 20 minutes or until the duck is tender. Stir in the rice, then begin adding the broth, a large ladle at a time, stirring gently until each ladle has almost been absorbed by the rice. The risotto should be kept at a bare simmer throughout cooking, so don't let the rice dry out—add more broth as necessary. Continue until the rice is tender and creamy, but the grains still firm. (This should take 15–20 minutes depending on the type of rice used—check the package instructions.)

Taste and season well with salt, pepper, and lemon juice, beat in the remaining butter, then stir in the spinach. Cover and let rest for a couple of minutes so the risotto can relax and the spinach wilt, then serve immediately. You may like to add a little more hot broth to the risotto just before you serve to loosen it, but don't let it wait around too long or the rice will turn mushy. Serve with freshly grated Parmesan cheese.

I was always excited when my father returned from a shoot with his game-bag full. Usually this meant pheasants, and this is one of the best ways to cook them. Roast pheasant is good too, but this is easier to eat and has all the wild, herby tastes of the hills.

pheasant and red wine risotto
risotto al fagiano e chianti

3 prepared pheasants or
6 boned pheasant breasts

about 6 cups hot Light Chicken Broth
or Game Broth (page 16)

2 bay leaves

1 stick unsalted butter

1 onion, finely chopped

1 carrot, finely chopped

1 celery stalk, finely chopped

¼ cup finely chopped pancetta or prosciutto

2½ cups risotto rice

1¼ cups red wine, such as Chianti

1 tablespoon chopped fresh thyme

¾ cup freshly grated Parmesan cheese

sea salt and freshly ground black pepper

chopped fresh parsley, to serve

Serves 6

Remove the breasts and legs from the pheasants and set aside. Cut up the carcass and add to the broth with the bay leaves. Simmer for 30 minutes before you start, then strain the broth into a pan and keep at simmering point on the top of the stove.

Pull the skin off the breasts and legs and cut the flesh into small pieces, discarding any bones. Melt half the butter in a large, heavy saucepan and add the onion, carrot, and celery (this is a *soffritto*). Cook gently for 10 minutes until soft and golden but not browned. Add the pancetta and pheasant and cook for another 5 minutes, but do not let it brown and harden. Stir in the rice until well coated with butter, heated through, and beginning to smell toasted. Pour in the wine, bring to a boil, and boil hard to reduce by half—this will concentrate the flavor and remove the raw taste of alcohol.

Begin adding the broth, a large ladle at a time, stirring gently until each ladle has almost been absorbed by the rice. The risotto should be kept at a bare simmer throughout cooking, so don't let the rice dry out—add more broth as necessary. Continue until the rice is tender and creamy, but the grains still firm. (This should take 15–20 minutes depending on the type of rice used—check the package instructions.)

Taste and season well with salt and pepper, then stir in the remaining butter, the thyme and Parmesan. Cover and let rest for a couple of minutes so the risotto can relax, then serve immediately, sprinkled with chopped parsley.

This is a rich and earthy risotto, redolent of the hills of Tuscany or Umbria in fall. Farm-reared rabbit is such good value, very tender with a better texture than chicken, but wild rabbit has more flavor. In this risotto, I use all the ingredients from the famous dish *Coniglio alla Cacciatora*.

hunter's-style rabbit risotto

risotto con coniglio alla cacciatora

about 6 cups hot Light Chicken Broth (page 16) or Vegetable Broth (page 15)

1 stick unsalted butter

1 onion, finely chopped

1 carrot, finely chopped

1 celery stalk, finely chopped

¼ cup finely chopped prosciutto

1¼ lb. rabbit meat, cut into small cubes

2⅓ cups risotto rice

1 tablespoon tomato purée

⅔ cup red wine, such as Chianti

1 tablespoon chopped fresh rosemary

3 cups mushrooms, cut into 4 pieces each

½ cup freshly grated Parmesan cheese

¼ cup Greek-style (dry-cured) black olives, pitted and quartered

sea salt and freshly ground black pepper

sprigs of rosemary, to serve

Serves 6

Put the broth in a saucepan and keep at a gentle simmer. Melt half the butter in a large, heavy saucepan and add the onion, carrot, and celery. Cook gently for 10 minutes until soft and golden but not browned. Add the prosciutto and rabbit and cook for another 5 minutes, but do not let it color and harden. Stir in the rice until well coated with butter, heated through, and beginning to smell toasted. Mix the tomato purée with the wine and pour onto the rice. Bring to a boil and boil hard to reduce by half—this will concentrate the flavor and remove the raw taste of alcohol. Stir in the rosemary.

Begin adding the broth, a large ladle at a time, stirring gently until each ladle has almost been absorbed by the rice. The risotto should be kept at a bare simmer throughout cooking, so don't let the rice dry out—add more broth as necessary. Halfway through cooking, stir in the mushrooms, then continue cooking, adding broth until the rice is tender and creamy, but the grains still firm. (This should take 15–20 minutes depending on the type of rice used—check the package instructions.)

Taste and season well with salt and pepper, then stir in the remaining butter, the Parmesan and the olives. Cover and let rest for a couple of minutes so the risotto can relax, then serve immediately, topped with rosemary sprigs.

meat and bacon

A real rib-sticker for the winter months. This risotto originates in the Val d'Aosta on the Italian-French border, where the pork spareribs are usually just simmered in broth until tender. This may not appeal to all, so I have tossed them in olive oil and balsamic vinegar and broiled them until crisp. They are then served on top of the risotto made with broccoli. Try to use purple-sprouting broccoli or broccolini, as these are both sweet and full of flavor.

broccoli risotto with spareribs
risotto con broccoli a modo mio

Beef or Veal Broth (page 19) – see method

2 lb. meaty spareribs, trimmed of any large amounts of fat

½ cup olive oil

3 tablespoons balsamic vinegar

risotto

1½ cups broccoli, trimmed and broken into florets

1 stick unsalted butter

1 onion, finely chopped

2 cups risotto rice

½ cup freshly grated Parmesan cheese

sea salt and freshly ground black pepper

3 tablespoons chopped fresh sage leaves, to serve

about 1.5 litres stock (see method)

aluminum foil

Serves 4

Follow the recipe for Beef or Veal Broth on page 19, substituting the spareribs for the beef and bones, simmering for 2 hours, and skimming often. Remove from the heat and lift out the spareribs. Chop up the ribs into manageable pieces. Put the oil and vinegar in a large bowl, whisk well, then add the ribs. Toss to coat, then set them in a foil-lined broiler pan. Heat the broiler and cook the spareribs for 10 minutes, turning and basting with the pan juices occasionally until browned and crisp. Keep them warm.

Strain the broth into a bowl through a colander lined with cheesecloth and discard the contents of the colander. Reserve the broth—you should have about 6 cups. Return the broth to the pan and return to simmering point. Add the broccoli and cook for 6–8 minutes or until tender. Remove with a slotted spoon and set aside. Melt half the butter in a large, heavy saucepan and add the onion. Cook gently for 10 minutes until soft, golden, and translucent but not browned. Add the rice and stir until well coated with the butter and heated through.

Begin adding the broth, a large ladle at a time, stirring gently until each ladle has almost been absorbed by the rice. The risotto should be kept at a bare simmer throughout cooking, so don't let the rice dry out—add more broth as necessary. Continue until the rice is tender and creamy, but the grains still firm. (This should take 15–20 minutes depending on the type of rice used—check the package instructions.)

Taste and season well with salt and pepper, beat in the remaining butter and fold in the broccoli. Cover and let rest for a couple of minutes so the risotto can relax and the broccoli heat through. Serve immediately with the spareribs piled on top, sprinkled with chopped sage. You may like to add a little more hot broth to the risotto just before you serve to loosen it, but don't let it wait around too long or the rice will turn mushy.

Italian sausages are pure pork—nothing added except salt and pepper and maybe chile or fennel seeds. They have a much better flavor than regular sausages, so it's worth seeking out a good Italian market in your area. In Italy, you choose your cut of pork and the sausages are made in moments right in front of you, leaving you to choose your own seasonings. Luganega is the long, coiled sausage and, if not fresh, can be bought vacuum-packed or sometimes by mail order.

risotto with italian sausages and roasted onions

risotto con salsicce e cipolle arrostite

about 6 cups hot Light Chicken Broth (page 16) or Vegetable Broth (page 15)

1 stick unsalted butter

1 lb. fresh Italian-style pork sausages, skins removed

1 onion, finely chopped

2 garlic cloves, finely chopped

⅔ cup Italian passata (strained crushed tomatoes)

2 teaspoons chopped fresh thyme

2½ cups risotto rice

¾ cup freshly grated Parmesan cheese, plus extra to serve

roasted onions

6 small whole red onions

½ cup olive oil

¼ cup balsamic vinegar

1 tablespoon chopped fresh thyme, plus extra sprigs to serve

sea salt and freshly ground black pepper

aluminum foil

Serves 6

To prepare the roasted onions, quarter them, then peel, keeping the root ends on to hold them together. Brush a roasting pan with a little olive oil and add the onions. Put the remaining olive oil, vinegar, thyme, salt, and pepper in a bowl, beat well, then brush over the onions, pouring any excess into the pan. Cover with foil and roast in a preheated oven at 400°F for 15 minutes. Remove the foil and roast for 10 minutes or until nicely caramelized. Remove from the oven and keep them warm.

To make the risotto, put the broth in a saucepan and keep at a gentle simmer. Melt half of the butter in a large, heavy saucepan and add the sausages. Cook over medium heat for 3–4 minutes, squashing with a spoon to break them up. Add the chopped onion and garlic and cook gently for 10 minutes until the onion is soft and golden. Add the passata and thyme and simmer for 5–10 minutes. Stir in the rice, making sure it is heated through before you add the broth.

Begin adding the broth, a large ladle at a time, stirring gently until each ladle has almost been absorbed by the rice. The risotto should be kept at a bare simmer throughout cooking, so don't let the rice dry out—add more broth as necessary. Continue until the rice is tender and creamy, but the grains still firm. (This should take 15–20 minutes depending on the type of rice used—check the package instructions.)

Taste and season well with salt and pepper, then beat in the remaining butter and all the Parmesan. Cover and let rest for a couple of minutes so the risotto can relax and the cheese melt. You may like to add a little more hot broth to the risotto just before you serve to loosen it, but don't let it wait around too long or the rice will turn mushy. Serve in warm bowls topped with the roasted onions and extra sprigs of thyme.

Once the staple food of the *gente di risaia*–the workers in the rice fields of Piemonte–this is a fantastic way to use any fresh beans in season. Although the quantity of salami used by the workers would have been small, I have used extra for a more affluent risotto. If you can't find fresh beans, use canned beans instead, and stir them in 5 minutes from the end of cooking to heat them through. Sometimes a glass of local Barolo would be added after the rice before the broth is added. This is a very soothing risotto.

salami and cranberry bean risotto

risotto con salame e fagioli borlotti

about 6 cups hot Beef or Veal Broth (page 19)

2 lb. fresh cranberry beans (or similar) in the pod, 3 cups shelled

1 stick unsalted butter

1 onion, finely chopped

6 oz. chunk of good salami, cubed

2 cups risotto rice, preferably carnaroli

¾ cup freshly grated Parmesan cheese, plus extra to serve

sea salt and freshly ground black pepper

Serves 6

Put the broth in a saucepan and keep at a gentle simmer. If using fresh beans, shell them and cook in the broth for about 20 minutes or until tender. Lift out with a slotted spoon and set aside.

Melt half of the butter in a large, heavy saucepan and add the onion. Cook gently for 10 minutes until soft, golden, and translucent but not browned. Stir in the salami and cook for 2 minutes. It must not brown. Add the rice and stir until well coated with the butter and heated through. Begin adding the broth, a large ladle at a time, stirring gently until each ladle has almost been absorbed by the rice. The risotto should be kept at a bare simmer throughout cooking, so don't let the rice dry out–add more broth as necessary. Continue until the rice is tender and creamy, but the grains still firm. (This should take 15–20 minutes depending on the type of rice used–check the package instructions.) Stir in the beans just before the risotto is ready.

Taste and season well with salt and pepper, then beat in the remaining butter and all the Parmesan cheese. Cover and let rest for a couple of minutes so the risotto can relax, then serve immediately. You may like to add a little more hot broth to the risotto just before you serve to loosen it, but don't let it wait around too long or the rice will turn mushy. Serve with extra grated Parmesan.

The leek is one of my favorite vegetables—it's not used enough. Its sweet, delicate, onion flavor is an excellent complement to salty cooked ham. Try to find ham sold in a piece so you can tear it into shreds—it will be more succulent than sliced ham. Roasting garlic softens and mellows the flavor until it is almost nutty.

ham and leek risotto
risotto con pancetta e porri

6 large garlic cloves

about ¾ cup olive oil

1 lb. leeks, plus 2 extra to serve

about 6 cups hot Light Chicken Broth (page 16)

2⅓ cups risotto rice

1 tablespoon grainy mustard

12 oz. cold ham, shredded, about 2 cups

½ cup freshly grated Parmesan cheese

sea salt and freshly ground black pepper

safflower oil, for cooking

Serves 4–6

Peel the garlic cloves and put them in a small saucepan. Cover with olive oil and heat to simmering. Simmer for about 20 minutes or until the garlic is golden and soft. Let cool in the oil.

Cut the 2 leeks into 3-inch lengths, then slice in half lengthwise and cut into long, thin shreds. Fill a wok or large saucepan one-third full with the safflower oil and heat to 375°F, add the shredded leeks, and deep-fry for 1 minute until crisp and just golden. Lift out of the oil, drain on paper towels, and set aside.

Slice the remaining leeks (thinly or thickly, as you like) into rounds. Put the broth in a saucepan and keep at a gentle simmer. Heat ⅓ cup of the garlic-flavored olive oil in a large, heavy saucepan. Add the leeks and sauté for a few minutes until beginning to soften and color slightly, then stir in the garlic cloves. Pour in the rice and stir until well coated with oil and heated through.

Begin adding the simmering broth, a large ladle at a time, stirring until each ladle has been absorbed by the rice. Continue until the rice is tender and creamy, but the grains still firm. Stir in the mustard and ham. Season well, stir in the Parmesan, cover, and let rest for a couple of minutes so the risotto can relax, before serving topped with a mound of fried leeks.

Here, a classic meat ragù is transformed into a creamy risotto. When making ragù, it is important not to brown the meat and vegetables too much—this will turn the meat into hard little bullets. It should brown just enough to turn from raw to cooked, then it will remain soft and homogenous. Cook the sauce very slowly, for as long as possible, 1–3 hours. The longer it simmers, the better it will taste. You can also make a big batch in a large covered casserole, then simmer in the oven at 300°F for 3 hours. Freeze what you don't use for later.

risotto with meat sauce
risotto al ragù

ragù

7 tablespoons unsalted butter

10 oz. lean ground beef, veal, or pork

¼ cup prosciutto with plenty of fat, ground or finely chopped

1 small onion, finely chopped

1 small carrot, finely chopped

1 celery stalk, finely chopped

3 tablespoons dry white wine

14 oz. canned tomato passata (Italian strained tomatoes) or puréed chopped tomatoes

1 tablespoon tomato purée or paste

about 2 quarts Beef or Veal Broth (page 19)

I bay leaf

sea salt and freshly ground black pepper

risotto

2⅓ cups risotto rice

¾ cup freshly grated Parmesan cheese, plus extra to serve

sea salt and freshly ground black pepper

Serves 6 generously

To make the ragù, melt half the butter in a heavy casserole dish over medium heat. Add the ground meat and prosciutto, onion, carrot, and celery. Brown very lightly (you are not trying to sear the meat, just turn it from pink to pale grey-brown). Make sure you break it up as it cooks so that there are no large lumps. Add the wine, turn up the heat, and boil until evaporated. Turn the heat down again. Add the tomato passata and purée, mix well, then add 2 cups broth, the bay leaf, salt, and pepper. Bring to a boil, stir well, then partially cover with a lid and reduce the heat to a bare simmer. Simmer for about 2 hours or until the butter begins to separate on the surface: it should be rich and thick. Add salt and pepper to taste.

Set the remaining broth on the stove and keep at a gentle simmer. Stir the rice into the ragù, mixing well. Increase to a simmer. Begin adding the broth, a large ladle at a time, stirring gently until each ladle has almost been absorbed by the rice. The risotto should be kept at a bare simmer throughout cooking, so don't let the rice dry out—add more broth as necessary. Continue until the rice is tender and creamy, but the grains still firm (15–20 minutes depending on the type of rice used—check the package instructions).

Taste and season well with salt and pepper, remove the bay leaf, and beat in the remaining butter and all the Parmesan. Cover and let rest for a couple of minutes so the risotto can relax and the cheese melt, then serve immediately. You may like to add a little more hot broth to the risotto just before you serve to loosen it, but don't let it wait around too long or the rice will turn mushy.

Artichokes are just made to go with lamb. Fresh, smaller artichokes with a purple blush are best here, but you can use pared-down globe artichokes, the char-grilled ones sold in Italian gourmet stores or even frozen artichoke bottoms or hearts. Canned artichokes are not so good.

risotto with lamb, artichokes, black olives, and garlic

risotto con agnello, carciofi e olive nere

12 fresh artichokes*, or 12 marinated artichokes, or 8 frozen artichoke hearts, thawed

butter, for sautéing (optional)

1 lb. lamb fillet, trimmed
(or a really well-trimmed rack of lamb—
no fat or gristle sticking to the bones)

1 tablespoon olive oil

about 6 cups hot Light Chicken (page 16),
Beef or Veal Broth (page 19),
or Vegetable Broth (page 15)

1 stick unsalted butter

2 shallots, finely chopped

1 celery stalk, finely chopped

1 small carrot, finely chopped

6 roasted garlic cloves (see Roasted Garlic Risotto with Goat Cheese and Rosemary on page 72)

2 cups risotto rice

⅔ cup fruity white wine

sea salt and freshly ground black pepper

to serve

20 Greek-style (dry-cured) black olives, pitted but left as large as possible

1 tablespoon finely chopped fresh marjoram

Serves 4

To prepare fresh young artichokes, see page 45.

First prepare the fresh artichokes, if using, then brush with olive oil and cook for 5 minutes on a stove-top grill pan, turning often, or slice the thawed artichoke bottoms and sauté in a little butter until golden.

Preheat the oven to 425°F. Heat an ovenproof skillet until very hot. Season the lamb well. Add the oil to the pan, then the lamb and a tablespoon of the butter, and cook over high heat for 2–3 minutes until well browned on all sides. Put the pan straight into the oven and roast for 7–12 minutes for the fillet (12–20 minutes for the rack), depending on how rare you like your meat. When cooked, lift out the lamb onto a heated plate, cover, and let it relax in a warm place while you make the risotto. Pour a ladle of the broth into the pan and deglaze, scraping up all the sediment. Set aside.

Put the broth in a saucepan and keep at a gentle simmer. Melt half the remaining butter in a large, heavy saucepan and add the shallots, celery, carrot, and roasted garlic cloves. Cook gently for 10 minutes until soft, golden, and translucent but not browned. Add the rice and stir until well coated with the butter and heated through. Pour in the wine and boil hard until it has reduced and almost disappeared. This will remove the taste of raw alcohol.

Add the pan juices from cooking the lamb, then begin adding the broth, a large ladle at a time, stirring gently until each ladle has almost been absorbed by the rice. The risotto should be kept at a bare simmer throughout cooking, so don't let the rice dry out—add more broth as necessary. Continue until the rice is tender and creamy, but the grains still firm (15–20 minutes depending on the type of rice used—check the package instructions).

Stir in the olives and marjoram, taste and season well with salt and pepper, then beat in all the remaining butter. Fold in the artichokes. Cover and let rest for a couple of minutes so the risotto can relax. Carve the meat into thick slices, then serve the risotto immediately, topped with the sliced lamb. You may like to add a little more hot broth to the risotto just before you serve to loosen it, but don't let the risotto wait around too long or the rice will turn mushy.

fish and seafood

One of my favorite risottos, this is stunning to look at. I love the rich iodine taste the ink gives to the sauce, and the sweetness of the squid or cuttlefish. Cleaned squid is available from most fishmongers. The all-important ink sacs have been packaged into little plastic sachets—find them in the refrigerator case at fishmongers. Using cuttlefish will give an immense amount of satisfaction and a stronger flavor to the risotto. Just for interest, *seppie* are cuttlefish, *calamari* are squid.

black risotto
risotto al nero di seppie

3 tablespoons extra virgin olive oil

½ onion, finely chopped

1 garlic clove, finely chopped

1¼ lb. cleaned squid, plus two sachets squid ink or 1 kg. whole cuttlefish (see below)

about 6 cups hot Fish Broth (page 20)

⅔ cup dry white wine

2⅓ cups risotto rice, preferably vialone nano

4 tablespoons unsalted butter, softened

2 tablespoon grappa (optional)

3 tablespoons finely chopped fresh flat-leaf parsley

sea salt and freshly ground black pepper

freshly grated Parmesan cheese, to serve (optional)

Serves 4–6

If using squid, cut body and tentacles into thin rings and small pieces. Keep some of the tentacles whole if you like. Heat the oil in a saucepan and add the onion and garlic. Cook gently for 10 minutes until soft, golden, and translucent but not browned. Add the squid, 2 ladles of broth, and the wine, then cover and cook gently for about 20 minutes or until tender, adding a little broth to the pan if necessary during cooking.

Add the rice and stir until well coated with the squid mixture and heated through. Mix the ink with a little broth and stir into the risotto. Begin adding the broth, a large ladle at a time, stirring gently until each ladle has almost been absorbed by the rice. The risotto should be kept at a bare simmer throughout cooking, so don't let the rice dry out—add more broth as necessary. Continue until the rice is tender and creamy and very *all'ondo* (liquid like a wave) but the grains still firm. (This should take 15–20 minutes depending on the type of rice used—check the package instructions.)

Taste and season well with salt and pepper, then beat in the butter and grappa, if using. Cover and let rest for a couple of minutes so the risotto can relax, then serve immediately topped with the chopped parsley, together with a bowl of Parmesan, if using.

Note To prepare fresh cuttlefish or squid, rinse it, then pull the tentacles and head away from the body. Carefully remove the silvery ink sacs from the heads without piercing them. Cut off all the internal organs still attached to the head. Put the ink sacs in a tea strainer over a small bowl and press out the ink with the back of a spoon. Cut through the thin skin covering the cuttlefish bone in the body and lift the bone out. Wash everything thoroughly in cold water and cut the body and tentacles into thin rings and small squares.

For those who aren't brave enough to try *risotto nero* made with squid ink, but still love squid, then this is for you. There is no sign of ink, just squid, garlic, wine, and parsley. You can make this with fresh or frozen prepared squid. If you have the tentacles, they make a great topping—just quickly sear them on a stove-top grill pan. I sometimes sauté a little extra sliced garlic and chopped red chile in olive oil and pour this over the risotto before serving.

white squid risotto
risotto bianco con calamari

about 6 cups hot Light Chicken Broth (page 16) or Vegetable Broth (page 15)

10 oz. fresh or frozen prepared squid (to prepare fresh squid or cuttlefish, see page 107)

1 stick unsalted butter

1 onion or 2 shallots, finely chopped

2–3 large garlic cloves, finely chopped

⅓ cup dry white wine

1½ cups risotto rice, preferably carnaroli

2 tablespoons chopped fresh parsley

1–2 tablespoons olive oil

sea salt and freshly ground black pepper

a stove-top grill pan or skillet

Serves 4

Put the broth in a saucepan and keep at a gentle simmer. Cut the squid into rings or small pieces and reserve the tentacles, if using. Melt half the butter in a large, heavy saucepan and add the onion or shallots and the garlic. Cook gently for 5 minutes until translucent but not browned. Add the squid, then the wine, and cook gently for 5 minutes, until the squid is white and the wine beginning to disappear. Add the rice and stir until well coated with the butter, wine and squid and heated through.

Begin adding the broth, a large ladle at a time, stirring gently until each ladle has almost been absorbed by the rice. The risotto should be kept at a bare simmer throughout cooking, so don't let the rice dry out—add more broth as necessary. Continue until the rice is tender and creamy, but the grains still firm. (This should take 15–20 minutes depending on the type of rice used—check the package instructions.)

Taste and season well with salt and pepper, then beat in the remaining butter and the parsley. Cover and let rest for a couple of minutes so the risotto can relax. Meanwhile heat a stove-top grill pan to smoking hot, toss the tentacles in the olive oil to coat, and add them to the pan. Cook for 1–2 minutes, then remove to a plate. Check the risotto—you may like to add a little more hot broth to the risotto just before you serve to loosen it, but don't let it wait around too long or the rice will turn mushy. Serve with the tentacles on top.

Make this risotto with whatever seafood you can find, but make it as varied as possible. Cooking the seafood in the broth before making the risotto will intensify its flavor. Italians do not generally serve grated Parmesan with seafood, so don't ask for any in a restaurant—it may be frowned on.

seafood risotto

risotto ai frutti di mare

8–16 oz. raw shell-on shrimp

6 cups hot Fish Broth (page 20)
or Quick Seafood Broth (page 20)

6 baby squid, cleaned, or 3 squid tubes

6 fresh sea (diver) scallops

1 lb. fresh mussels

10 oz. small fresh clams

6 tablespoons unsalted butter

1 onion, finely chopped

2⅓ cups risotto rice, preferably carnaroli

1¼ cups dry white wine

sea salt and freshly ground black pepper

3 tablespoons chopped fresh parsley, to serve

Serves 6 generously

Pull off the shrimp heads and put them in the broth with the wine, bring to a boil, cover, and simmer for 20 minutes. Cut the squid into rings and trim the tentacles. Remove the hard white muscle, if any, from the side of each scallop. Scrub the mussels well and pull off any beards. Discard any that don't close when sharply tapped against a work surface. Rinse the clams well.

Strain the broth into a clean pan and heat to simmering point. Add the shrimps and cook for 2 minutes. Add the squid and scallops and cook for a further 2 minutes. Remove them all with a slotted spoon and set aside. Put the mussels and clams into the broth and bring to a boil. Cover and cook for 5 minutes or until all the shellfish have opened. Remove with a slotted spoon and set aside.

Melt the butter in a large, heavy saucepan and add the onion. Cook gently for 10 minutes until softened but not browned. Pour in the rice and stir until well coated with butter and heated through. Add the wine and bring to a boil. Boil fast until reduced by half.

Begin adding the hot broth, a large ladle at a time, stirring until each ladle has been absorbed by the rice. Continue until all but 2 ladles of broth are left, and the rice is tender but still has some bite to it, 15–20 minutes.

Taste and season well with salt and pepper. Finally stir in the remaining broth and all the seafood and cook gently with the lid on for 5 minutes or until piping hot. The risotto shouldn't be too thick. Transfer to a large warmed bowl and sprinkle with the parsley. Serve immediately.

Fresh crab makes a delicious risotto, especially when speckled with fresh red chile. Although fresh crab is preferable, it's a bit fiddly to prepare and you can buy frozen crabmeat which is very acceptable for this recipe.

crab and chile risotto

risotto al granchio e peperoncino

about 6 cups hot Quick Seafood Broth or Fish Broth (page 20), or Vegetable Broth (page 15)

7 tablespoons unsalted butter

3 shallots, finely chopped

2 celery stalks, finely chopped

2 cups risotto rice

1 fresh red chile, seeded and finely chopped

1 bay leaf

⅔ cup dry white wine

8 oz. crabmeat, fresh or frozen and thawed, (1½ cups)

sea salt and freshly ground black pepper

4–8 meaty crab claws, cooked and cracked (optional)

¼ cup chopped fresh flat-leaf parsley

Serves 4

Put the broth in a saucepan and keep at a gentle simmer. Melt half the butter in a large, heavy saucepan and add the shallots and celery. Cook gently for 5–7 minutes until soft, golden, and translucent but not browned. Add the rice, chopped chile, and bay leaf, stir until well coated with the butter, translucent, and heated through. Pour in the wine and boil hard until it has reduced and almost disappeared. This will remove the taste of raw alcohol.

Begin adding the broth, a large ladle at a time, stirring gently until each ladle has almost been absorbed by the rice. The risotto should be kept at a bare simmer throughout cooking, so don't let the rice dry out—add more broth as necessary. Continue until the rice is tender and creamy, but the grains still firm. (This should take 15–20 minutes depending on the type of rice used—check the package instructions.)

Five minutes before the rice is ready, stir in half the crabmeat. When the rice is cooked, taste and season well with salt and pepper, then stir in the remaining butter. Remove the bay leaf. Fold in the remaining crabmeat, being careful not to break up any lumps. Cover and let rest for a couple of minutes so the risotto can relax, then serve immediately. Serve topped with the crab claws, if using, and lots of chopped fresh parsley.

This is a quick way to cook a special risotto. Adding pounded shells of the lobster to a vegetable broth will improve the flavor. If making this with shrimp, cook them first, peel them, then pound the shells and add to the broth. Add the chopped shrimp where you would the lobster flesh.

lobster or shrimp risotto

risotto all'aragosta o gamberi

about 6 cups hot Quick Seafood Broth (page 20) or Vegetable Broth (page 15)

2 medium cooked lobsters, about 1–1¼ lb. each, or 2–2½ lb. shrimp

1 stick unsalted butter

2 shallots, finely chopped

2⅓ cups risotto rice

3 tablespoons sweet red vermouth

sea salt and freshly ground black pepper

fresh lemon juice

a pinch of cayenne, to serve

Serves 6

Put the broth in a saucepan and keep at a gentle simmer. Split the lobsters in half and remove the stomach sac and long intestine. Prise out the tail meat and any red coral or roe and set aside. Crack the claws and extract the meat and set aside. Put all the shells including the heads into a solid bowl and pound them with the end of a rolling pin until they are broken into small fragments. Add these to the broth and simmer for 30 minutes. Cut the lobster meat into chunks and chop up the roe. Pour the broth through a fine strainer and return to the heat. Discard the contents of the strainer.

Melt half the butter in a large, heavy saucepan and add the shallots. Cook gently for 5 minutes until soft, golden, and translucent but not browned. Add the rice and stir until well coated with the butter and heated through. Pour in the vermouth and boil hard until it has reduced and almost disappeared. This will remove the taste of raw alcohol.

Begin adding the broth, a large ladle at a time, stirring gently until each ladle has almost been absorbed by the rice. The risotto should be kept at a bare simmer throughout cooking, so don't let the rice dry out—add more broth as necessary. Continue until the rice is tender and creamy, but the grains still firm. (This should take 15–20 minutes depending on the type of rice used—check the package instructions.)

Taste and season well with salt, pepper, and lemon juice, beat in the remaining butter and reserved roe, and gently fold in the lobster meat. Cover and let rest for a couple of minutes so the risotto can relax and the lobster heat through, then serve immediately. You may like to add a little more hot broth to the risotto just before you serve to loosen it, but don't let it wait around too long or the rice will turn mushy. Serve sprinkled with a little cayenne.

Cooking this rich risotto with dry vermouth instead of wine gives it a certain finesse and a herbal note. I often use a little dry vermouth when cooking fish and seafood when I don't have any wine open.

scallop and scallion risotto
risotto con capesante e cipollotti

about 6 cups Hot Seafood Broth or Fish Broth (page 20) or Vegetable Broth (page 15)

12 large fresh or frozen sea scallops

1 stick unsalted butter

6 scallions, sliced or chopped—white and green parts kept separate

2 cups risotto rice, preferably carnaroli

⅓ cup dry white vermouth

sea salt and freshly ground black pepper

Serves 4

Put the broth in a saucepan and keep at a gentle simmer. Look at the scallops and check to see if there is a tiny tough white muscle clinging to the side—if there is, pull off and discard. Slice each scallop in half around the middle. Set aside. Melt half the butter in a large, heavy saucepan and, when foaming, sauté the scallops quickly, browning them on both sides. Remove to a plate before they overcook: they will only take 2 minutes at the most. Add the white part of the scallions and cook gently for 3–4 minutes until soft, golden, and translucent but not browned.

Add the rice and stir until well coated with the butter and heated through. Pour in the vermouth and boil hard to reduce and almost disappeared. This will remove the taste of raw alcohol.

Begin adding the broth, a large ladle at a time, stirring gently until each ladle has almost been absorbed by the rice. The risotto should be kept at a bare simmer throughout cooking, so don't let the rice dry out—add more broth as necessary. Continue until the rice is tender and creamy, but the grains still firm. (This should take 15–20 minutes depending on the type of rice used—check the package instructions.)

Taste and season well with salt and pepper, beat in the remaining butter, and fold in the scallops and green parts of the scallions. Cover and let rest for a couple of minutes so the risotto can relax and the scallops heat through, then serve immediately. You may like to add a little more hot broth to the risotto just before you serve to loosen it, but don't let it wait around too long or the rice will turn mushy and the scallops will overcook.

Though it still tastes luxurious, the ingredients for this risotto are regular pantry ingredients. Canned smoked fish is a wonderful standby—for extra flavor, keep the oil and use it instead of the butter for softening the vegetables. A hint of tarragon is always good with smoky things, as is the sweetness of the leeks. This would also work well with flakes of any smoked fish such as mackerel or finnan haddie (smoked haddock).

smoked mussel or oyster and leek risotto
risotto con cozze o ostriche affumicate

about 6 cups hot Vegetable Broth (page 15)

1 stick unsalted butter

1 large leek, finely sliced or chopped (all the white part and half of the green)

1 celery stalk, finely chopped

2 cups risotto rice, preferably carnaroli

⅛ cup dry white vermouth

1 teaspoon chopped fresh tarragon

3 cans smoked mussels or oysters, 3 oz. each, drained

sea salt and freshly ground black pepper

Serves 4

Put the broth in a saucepan and keep at a gentle simmer. Melt half the butter in a large, heavy saucepan and, when foaming, add the sliced leeks and celery and cook gently for 5 minutes until softened but not browned. Add the rice and stir until well coated with the butter and heated through. Pour in the vermouth and boil hard until reduced and almost disappeared. This will remove the taste of raw alcohol. Add the tarragon.

Begin adding the broth, a large ladle at a time, stirring gently until each ladle has almost been absorbed by the rice. The risotto should be kept at a bare simmer throughout cooking, so don't let the rice dry out—add more broth as necessary. Continue until the rice is tender and creamy, but the grains still firm. (This should take 15–20 minutes depending on the type of rice used—check the package instructions.)

Taste and season well with salt and pepper, beat in the remaining butter, and fold in the smoked mussels or oysters. Cover and let rest for a couple of minutes so the risotto can relax and the seafood heat through, then serve immediately. You may like to add a little more hot broth to the risotto just before you serve to loosen it, but don't let it wait around too long or the rice will turn mushy and the seafood will overcook.

A simple risotto relying on the freshness and delicate flavors of the mussels or clams. Smaller mussels or clams are always the sweetest, so choose them instead of big fat ones. The secret is not to overcook the mussel or clam meat, so steam them until just opened, then strain immediately. Try to strain the resulting cooking liquid through a fine tea strainer or cheesecloth, because clams and mussels can be gritty. This should be quite a loose risotto.

mussel or clam risotto
risotto con cozze o vongole

3 lb. live mussels or small clams

about 6 cups hot Fish Broth (page 20) or Vegetable Broth (page 15)

1 stick unsalted butter

1 small onion, finely chopped

2 garlic cloves, finely chopped

2⅓ cups risotto rice, preferably vialone nano

sea salt and freshly ground black pepper

3 tablespoons chopped fresh flat-leaf parsley

Serves 6

Discard any mussels or clams with broken shells, or any that are open and will not close when sharply tapped against a surface. Wash and scrub them thoroughly, pulling off any beards, then leave them to soak in cold water for 1 hour to purge them. Drain and transfer to a large saucepan over high heat, with no extra water other than whatever is still clinging to them. Cover and steam for 2–5 minutes (2–3 for clams, 4–5 for mussels), until they open fully, giving the pan a shake now and then. Strain them through a colander and reserve the cooking liquid. When cool enough to handle, remove the flesh from the shells, leaving a few in the shell for serving. Strain the resulting liquid through a very fine strainer or cheesecloth.

Put the broth in a saucepan and keep at a gentle simmer. Melt half the butter in a large, heavy saucepan and add the onion and garlic. Cook gently for 10 minutes until soft, golden, and translucent but not browned. Add the rice and stir until well coated with the butter and heated through. Stir in the strained mussel liquid. When this has been absorbed, begin adding the broth, a large ladle at a time, stirring gently until each ladle has almost been absorbed by the rice. The risotto should be kept at a bare simmer throughout cooking, so don't let the rice dry out—add more broth as necessary. Continue until the rice is tender and creamy, but the grains still firm. (This should take 15–20 minutes depending on the type of rice used—check the package instructions.)

Taste and season well with salt and pepper, beat in the remaining butter, and gently fold in the cooked mussels or clams and 2 tablespoons of the parsley. Cover and let rest for a few minutes so the risotto can relax and the shellfish heat through, then serve immediately topped with the remaining parsley and the reserved mussels in their shells. You may like to add a little more hot broth to the risotto just before you serve to loosen it, but don't let it wait around too long or the rice will turn mushy.

The fresh and slightly musky flavor of capers is delicious in a fish risotto, especially if they are salted capers, which are more pungent than the ones in vinegar. The tuna in this recipe is cut thicker than normal by Italian standards and broiled until crusty on the outside, but pink and tender inside. Masked with a fresh, vibrant sauce from Sicily, this is perfect for a summer meal.

caper risotto with grilled tuna and salmoriglio sauce

risotto con capperi, tonno e salmoriglio

4 tuna steaks, cut 1-inch thick

about ⅓ cup extra virgin olive oil

sea salt and freshly ground black pepper

salmoriglio sauce

finely grated zest and juice of
½ large unwaxed lemon, or to taste

a pinch of sugar

¼ cup extra-virgin olive oil

1 garlic clove, finely chopped

2 teaspoons dried (not fresh) oregano

2 tablespoons fresh mint, finely chopped

caper risotto

about 6 cups hot Fish Broth (page 20)
or Vegetable Broth (page 15)

1 onion, finely chopped

2⅓ cups risotto rice

⅔ cup dry white wine

¼ cup capers in salt, rinsed,
then soaked for 10 minutes in warm water

finely grated zest and juice of
1 unwaxed lemon, to taste

sea salt and freshly ground black pepper

aluminum foil

Serves 4

To make the salmoriglio sauce, put the lemon juice and sugar in a bowl, stir to dissolve, then add the lemon zest. Whisk in ¼ cup of the olive oil, then stir in the garlic, oregano and chopped mint. Set aside to infuse.

Preheat the broiler or outdoor grill. Brush the tuna with 2 tablespoons olive oil and season with salt and pepper. Set on a rack in a foil-lined broiler pan. Broil or grill for about 1–2 minutes on each side until crusty on the outside and still pink in the middle. Remove the fish from the heat, cover, and keep it warm while you make the risotto.

Put the broth in a saucepan and keep at a gentle simmer. Heat ¼ cup olive oil in a large, heavy saucepan and add the onion. Cook gently for 10 minutes until soft, golden, and translucent but not browned. Add the rice and stir until well coated with the oil and heated through. Add the wine and boil hard until it has reduced and almost disappeared. This will remove the taste of raw alcohol.

Begin adding the broth, a large ladle at a time, stirring gently until each ladle has almost been absorbed by the rice. The risotto should be kept at a bare simmer throughout cooking, so don't let the rice dry out—add more broth as necessary. Continue until the rice is tender and creamy, but the grains still firm. (This should take 15–20 minutes depending on the type of rice used—check the package instructions.)

Taste and season well with salt and pepper, chopped capers, lemon juice, and zest to taste. Cover and let rest for a couple of minutes so the risotto can relax. You may like to add a little more hot broth to the risotto just before you serve to loosen it, but don't let it wait around too long or the rice will turn mushy. Slice the tuna steaks. Spoon the risotto onto warm plates and set the sliced tuna on top of each. Spoon the sauce over the top and serve.

Smoked salmon has become very fashionable in Italy and I have even seen it on pizzas—overcooked and not very pleasant. However, smoked salmon is sublime in a very creamy risotto enriched with butter, cream, and Parmesan (one of the few times it is respectable to use Parmesan in a fish or seafood risotto). This risotto should be quite liquid.

smoked salmon risotto

risotto cremoso con salmone affumicato

about 6 cups hot Fish Broth (page 20) or Vegetable Broth (page 15)

1 stick unsalted butter

3 shallots, very finely chopped

1 garlic clove, finely chopped

1½ cups risotto rice

⅓ cup dry vermouth

¼ cup heavy cream or 2 tablespoons mascarpone cheese

½ cup finely grated Parmesan cheese, plus extra to serve

8 oz. sliced smoked salmon, cut into thin strips

2 tablespoons chopped fresh dill

finely grated zest and juice of 1 unwaxed lemon

sea salt and freshly ground black pepper

Serves 4

Put the broth in a saucepan and keep at a gentle simmer. Melt half the butter in a large, heavy saucepan and add the shallots and garlic. Cook gently for 10 minutes until soft, golden, and translucent but not browned. Add the rice and stir until well coated with the butter and heated through. Pour in the vermouth and boil hard to reduce and almost disappeared. This will remove the taste of raw alcohol.

Begin adding the broth, a large ladle at a time, stirring gently until each ladle has almost been absorbed by the rice. The risotto should be kept at a bare simmer throughout cooking, so don't let the rice dry out—add more broth as necessary. Continue until the rice is tender and creamy, but the grains still firm. (This should take 15–20 minutes depending on the type of rice used—check the package instructions.)

Taste and season well with salt and pepper, then beat in the remaining butter, the cream, and Parmesan. Gently fold in half the salmon, and all the dill and lemon zest. Cover and let rest for a couple of minutes so the risotto can relax and the flavors develop. Taste again and season with lemon juice, then serve immediately. You may like to add a little more hot broth to the risotto just before you serve to loosen it, but don't let it wait around too long or the rice will turn mushy. Top with the remaining smoked salmon.

other ways with risotto

Barlotto is one of my friend Nick Nairn's specialities. He loves to make this in fall after mushroom-hunting near his cooking school on the Lake of Menteith in Scotland.

I have always loved the chewy nuttiness of this recipe, and thought the title was a bit of a pun on the words barley and risotto, but have recently found out that a similar dish is made in Venezia-Friuli-Giulia called *orzotto*. To make serving this dish easier, Nick suggests making the barlotto in advance and reheating it—something it does well, because unlike rice, barley doesn't go soggy with keeping.

barlotto with red wine and mushrooms
orzotto al vino rosso e funghi

3 tablespoons olive oil

¾ cup plus 2 tablespoons pearl barley, washed and drained

1 small onion, finely chopped

1 garlic clove, finely chopped

2 cups hot Light Chicken Broth (page 16), Vegetable Broth (page 15) or water

1 tablespoon light soy sauce

⅔ cup red wine

10 oz. fresh chanterelles (or other wild and cultivated mushrooms, such as porcini or portobellos)

6 tablespoons unsalted butter

2 tablespoons chopped fresh parsley

1 tablespoon chopped fresh tarragon

sea salt and freshly ground black pepper

aluminum foil

Serves 4

Heat the oil in a large saucepan, then add the barley and stir until it starts to turn golden (not brown)—this will take about 5 minutes. Add the onion and garlic and continue sautéing until the barley starts to brown, 5–10 minutes. Don't let it burn, but you want a good, toasted flavor.

Add the broth, soy sauce, red wine, salt, and pepper. Bring to a boil, reduce the heat, partially cover with a lid, then simmer gently until nearly all the liquid has been absorbed—this should take at least 30 minutes. The beauty of this one is that you don't need to stir it constantly.

Meanwhile, brush or scrape the mushrooms clean (slicing any bigger ones to size) and heat a skillet until hot. Add 4 tablespoons of the butter, then the mushrooms. Stir-fry over medium heat until lightly browned, 4–5 minutes. Season with salt and pepper. Add the stir-fried mushrooms to the barley and mix gently. Remove from the heat and cover with kitchen foil with a few holes pierced in it to let the barley swell and absorb all the liquid. Leave it in a warm place for 15 minutes. (At this stage, you could let the barlotto cool, reheating it for serving up to 24 hours later.)

To serve, put the barlotto pan back on the heat and beat in the parsley, tarragon, and the remaining 2 tablespoons of butter. Stir well until hot, add salt and pepper to taste and pile onto heated plates. Serve immediately.

Supplì are real comfort food. When you bite one, you can pull the melted oozing mozzarella into strings that are said to look like telephone wires strung from pole to pole—hence the name, *supplì al telefono*. You can make it with leftover risotto, but it is so good (children adore it), it is worth making from scratch as a appetizer or a snack.

rice croquettes with tomato sauce
supplì al telefono con sugo di pomodoro

tomato sauce

½ cup olive oil

2 garlic cloves, chopped

1 teaspoon dried (not fresh) oregano

1¾ lb. fresh tomatoes, peeled and coarsely chopped, or 28 oz. canned chopped tomatoes

sea salt and freshly ground black pepper

supplì

2 eggs, lightly beaten

⅓ recipe Parmesan and Butter Risotto (page 63)

4 oz. mozzarella cheese balls, cut into 20 cubes

2 slices of cooked ham or mortadella, cut into 20 strips

⅔ cup dried white bread crumbs, for coating

sea salt and freshly ground black pepper

oil, for deep-frying

Makes 20

To make the tomato sauce, heat the oil almost to smoking point in a large, shallow pan or wok. Standing back (it will splutter if it's at the right temperature), add the garlic, oregano, tomatoes, and pepper. To acquire its distinctive, concentrated, almost caramelized flavor, the tomatoes must sauté at a very lively heat in a shallow pan, so cook over fierce heat for 5-8 minutes or until the sauce is thick and glossy. Add salt to taste, pass through a food mill or blend in a food processor, then strain to remove the seeds. Set aside.

Beat the eggs into the risotto. Spread the mixture out on a plate and let cool completely, about 1 hour.

Take a large spoonful of risotto and, with damp hands, mold it into an egg shape. Insert your little finger down through the top of the egg but not quite to the bottom, to make a hole inside. Push in a cube of cheese wrapped with a strip of ham and pinch the top over. Roll the egg shape into a fat cylinder, making sure the filling doesn't burst through. Set on a tray while you make the others. Put the bread crumbs in a shallow bowl. Roll the *supplì* in the bread crumbs until evenly coated. At this stage they can be covered and left in the refrigerator for up to 1 day.

Heat the oil in a large saucepan until a crumb will sizzle immediately—350°F. Fry 3–4 at a time for 4–5 minutes until deep golden. Drain on paper towels, sprinkle with salt and serve immediately with warm tomato sauce (or keep warm in a low oven for up to 15 minutes).

These cocktail-sized mouthfuls can be refrigerated for up to a day, ready to sauté at the last moment. They will keep warm in a low oven for 30 minutes—but keep them covered and don't add a topping until the last minute. Deep-fried basil leaves are crisply translucent and make a beautiful topping. To cook them, heat oil in a deep-fryer to 375°F. Make sure the basil leaves are dry, then put in the basket. Fry for 30 seconds—they will hiss alarmingly. Remove immediately and drain on paper towels. They will crisp more on cooling.

little tomato risotto cakes
saltimbocca di risotto

2 cups Vegetable Broth (page 15)

2 cups tomato juice or mixed vegetable juice, such as V8

3 tablespoons olive oil

1 small onion, finely chopped

1 garlic clove, finely chopped

1 heaping cup risotto rice, preferably arborio

⅔ cup dry white wine

¼ cup sun-dried tomato paste or tomato paste

4 oz. sun-blushed tomatoes, chopped*

½ cup freshly grated Parmesan cheese

1 small egg, beaten

sea salt and freshly ground black pepper

32 fresh basil leaves, plus extra to serve

16 paperthin slices of pancetta, halved

sea salt and freshly ground black pepper

Makes about 32

If you are unable to find sun-blushed tomatoes, buy 8 oz. organic grape tomatoes and semi-dry them in a preheated oven at 250°F for about 1 hour.

Put the broth and tomato or vegetable juice in a saucepan and keep at a gentle simmer. Heat the olive oil in a large, heavy saucepan and add the onion. Cook gently for 5 minutes, then add the garlic and cook for a further 5 minutes until soft, golden, and translucent but not browned. Add the rice, then stir until well coated with the oil and heated through. Pour in the wine and boil hard until it has reduced and almost disappeared. This will remove the taste of raw alcohol. Stir in the sun-dried tomato paste.

Add the broth, a large ladle at a time, stirring gently until each ladle has almost been absorbed by the rice. The risotto should be kept at a bare simmer throughout cooking, so don't let the rice dry out—add more broth as necessary. Continue until the rice is tender and creamy, and thicker than normal. (This should take about 20 minutes depending on the type of rice used—check the package instructions.) Stir in the sun-blushed tomatoes and Parmesan.

Taste and season well with salt and pepper, then beat in the egg. Spread out the mixture on a tray until cool enough to handle, about 30 minutes. Roll into bite-size balls with damp hands, flatten, set on a tray, and cover with plastic wrap. Leave to firm up in the refrigerator. When firm, put a basil leaf on top of each one and wrap with a strip of pancetta. Heat a little oil in a nonstick skillet and sauté for about 1 minute on each side until golden. Serve warm, topped with fresh or quickly deep-fried basil leaves (see recipe introduction).

These crisp golden balls, stuffed with leftover meat ragù, are eaten as street food in Sicily. However, made cocktail snack size, they are perfect to serve with drinks. Unlike making a true risotto, you should overcook the rice to make it really stick together. The mixture should be very thick before it is cooled and can be made with leftover risotto.

arancine di riso

6 tablespoons unsalted butter

1 onion, finely chopped

⅔ cup dry white wine

1⅓ cups risotto rice, preferably arborio

1 quart hot Vegetable Broth (page 15) or Light Chicken Broth (page 16)

8 saffron threads or ¼ teaspoon powdered saffron

¼ cup freshly grated Parmesan cheese

1 medium egg

about 1 cup meat ragù (page 101), or use leftover ragù

sea salt and freshly ground black pepper

oil, for deep-frying

coating

⅔ cup all purpose flour

2 extra-large eggs, beaten

¾ cup dry white bread crumbs

an electric deep-fryer or wok

Serves 4–6

Melt the butter in a large, heavy saucepan and add the onion. Cook gently for 10 minutes until soft and golden but not browned. Pour in the wine and boil hard until reduced and almost disappeared. Stir in the rice and coat with the butter and wine. Add a ladle of broth and the saffron and simmer, stirring until absorbed. Continue adding the broth, ladle by ladle, until all the broth has been absorbed. The rice should be very tender, thick, and golden. (This should take about 20 minutes).

Taste and season well with salt and pepper, then stir in the Parmesan. Lightly whisk the egg and beat into the risotto. Spread out on a plate and let cool completely, about 1 hour. Take 1 tablespoon cold risotto and, with damp hands, spread out in the palm of one hand. Mound a small teaspoon of meat ragù in the center. Take another tablespoon of risotto and set over the ragù to enclose it completely. Carefully roll and smooth in your hands to form a perfect round ball (or form into a cone shape with a rounded end). Continue until all the risotto and filling has been used.

To make the coating, put the flour on a plate, the beaten egg in a shallow dish, and the bread crumbs in a shallow bowl. Roll the arancine first in the flour, then in the egg, and finally roll in the bread crumbs until evenly coated. At this stage, they can be covered and left in the refrigerator for up to 1 day.

Heat the oil in a deep-fryer or wok until a crumb will sizzle immediately— 350°F. Fry a few arancine at a time for 3–5 minutes until deep golden. Drain on paper towels, sprinkle with salt, and serve immediately (or keep warm in a low oven for up to 15 minutes).

Note For vegetarians, instead of the meat ragù filling, use 3 oz. finely chopped mozzarella, 4 sun-dried tomatoes in oil, drained and finely chopped, and a few finely chopped fresh basil leaves.

This is my version of Sweet Risotto Cake (*torta di riso dolce*), so popular throughout Italy. The cooked rice is often mixed with candied fruits and nuts, but this is not to everyone's taste, so I mix in amarena cherries (a great favorite of mine), ground almonds and pistachios. Normally this is cooked in a 10-inch cake pan and tends to be a bit dry, so I cook them individually and serve with amarena syrup poured over the top. Amarena cherries are available in pretty blue and white glass jars or in less expensive cans.

cherry and almond risotto puddings

budini di riso con amarene e mandorle

¾ cup risotto rice, ideally vialone nano

4 cups whole milk

2 tablespoons semolina

14 oz. canned amarena cherries, plus extra to serve

6 eggs

¾ cup sugar

½ cup slivered almonds, ground to a powder in a blender*

grated zest of 1 unwaxed lemon

3 tablespoons maraschino liqueur or brandy

⅓ cup pistachios, halved

6–8 ramekins or dariole molds, lightly buttered, then dusted with semolina

a baking sheet

Serves 6–8

Put the rice and the milk in a saucepan. Slowly bring to a boil, reduce the heat, and simmer for 15 minutes. Drain the cherries and reserve the syrup. Halve the cherries, rinse, and dry on paper towels.

Put the eggs, sugar, ground almonds, lemon zest, and liqueur in a large bowl and beat until pale and creamy. Fold into the rice, then fold in the halved cherries and pistachios. Spoon into the molds and level the tops. Set the filled molds on the baking sheet and bake in a preheated oven at 350°F for about 25 minutes or until a wooden skewer inserted in the center comes out clean. The puddings should be set and golden brown.

Let cool in the molds for 5 minutes, then run a knife around the edge to loosen. Invert onto serving plates. Serve warm or cold with the reserved cherry syrup and extra cherries.

Note When grinding almonds, put them in the freezer for 30 minutes, then grind them in a food processor using the pulse button. This will prevent them becoming oily.

A delicious creamy risotto based on an ancient recipe from the northeast coast of Sicily. Chocolate arrived in Sicily from the New World via the court of Spain. The Spanish used it as a drink and a flavoring ingredient. It is still made in Modica today and is slightly grainy and not over-processed, retaining its ancient roots. It is variously flavored with vanilla, cinnamon, and chile (a flavor beloved by Sicilians). A pinch of ground red pepper in the dessert adds a warmth and mysterious flavor—for adults only.

dark chocolate risotto

riso nero

3 tablespoons unsweetened cocoa powder

½ cup sugar

¼ teaspoon ground cinnamon

4 cups whole milk

¾ cup risotto rice, preferably vialone nano

3 long strips of orange zest

3½ oz. bittersweet chocolate, grated

½ cup chopped candied orange peel (optional)

to serve

cinnamon sticks

candied orange peel

confectioners' sugar

light cream

Serves 4

Put the cocoa powder, sugar, and cinnamon in a small bowl and add ¼ cup of the milk. Mix until well blended, then add another ¼ cup milk.

Put the rice in a medium saucepan and stir in the cocoa-flavored milk, the remaining milk and the strips of orange zest. Slowly bring to a boil, then reduce the heat, cover, and barely simmer for 20 minutes. The rice should be very tender, creamy, and slightly sloppy (if not, add a little extra hot milk). Remove the strips of orange zest and stir in the chocolate until it has completely melted, then the candied orange peel, if using.

Spoon into 4 small warm bowls or glass heatproof dishes and set a cinnamon stick and a slice of candied peel in each one. Sprinkle with confectioners' sugar, serve immediately with light cream and eat while still warm.

Sounds crazy, but this is a delicate, creamy vanilla ice cream, with an interesting granular texture. I love it. Its origins seem to be in Moorish Sicily, where rosewater, cinnamon, and even ginger were used as flavorings. It has now become popular all over Italy. Tiny, wild strawberries, cherries cooked in red wine, fresh peaches marinated in sweet wine, or warm roasted figs—all go perfectly with this ice cream. It is ambrosial served with rose petal jam.

rice ice cream
gelato di riso

½ cup Italian arborio rice

1¼ cups whole milk

1 vanilla bean, split

¾ cup plus 2 tablespoons sugar

2¾ cups heavy cream, chilled
(or 8 oz. mascarpone cheese
mixed with 1¼ cups milk until smooth)

1 tablespoon orange flower water or rose water

wax paper or plastic wrap

an electric ice cream maker

Serves 8

Put the rice in a flameproof casserole with the milk and vanilla bean. Bring to a boil, cover tightly, bake in a preheated oven at 350°F for about 1 hour until very tender. (Alternatively, simmer on top of the stove for 30 minutes until tender.) When cooked, discard the vanilla bean (rinsing and drying it to put in a jar of sugar later), stir in the sugar, and cover the surface with wax paper or plastic wrap.

Let cool, then chill in the refrigerator for at least 1 hour. When cold, stir in the cream (or mascarpone and milk) and orange flower water or rosewater. Freeze in an ice cream maker according to the manufacturer's instructions until it is the consistency of whipped cream, then transfer to a freezerproof container and keep in the freezer for at least 2 hours. Transfer the ice cream to the refrigerator 1 hour before serving, to soften. Serve in soft scoops, with peaches, figs, or cherries.

Notes

If you do not have an ice cream machine, freeze the mixture in a freezerproof container, whisking periodically during freezing to break down the ice crystals and ensure a smooth-textured result.

If making double quantity, 4 cups cream is enough.

websites and mail order

GROW YOUR OWN

The Cook's Garden
PO Box C5030
Warminster, PA 18974
800-457-9703
www.cooksgarden.com
An excellent resource for the kitchen gardener. Many of their seeds are certified organic.

KITCHEN EQUIPMENT

Bed Bath & Beyond
1-800-462-3966
www.bedbathandbeyond.com

Bridge Kitchenware
711 Third Avenue
New York, NY 10017
212-688-4200
customerservice@bridgekitchenware.com
www.bridgekitchenware.com

Chef's Catalog
800-338-3232
www.chefscatalog.com

Crate & Barrel
800-967-6696
www.crateandbarrel.com

Sur la Table
800-243-0852
www.surlatable.com

Williams-Sonoma
877-812-6235
www.williams-sonoma.com

ITALIAN FOOD

Baroni
Mercato Centrale, Florence, Italy
www.baronialimentari.it
The Baroni family offers top-quality condiments, oils, aged balsamic vinegars, fresh alpine butter, fresh black and white truffles in season, and truffle products and will ship all over the world. Visit when in Florence, or visit the site to be transported.

ChefShop.com
800-596-0885
P.O. Box 3488
Seattle, WA 98114
www.chefshop.com
Features a wide range of quality raw ingredients, plus condiments and seasonings.

Dean and DeLuca
800-221-7714
www.deandeluca.com

Esperya
www.esperya.com
Genuine, high-quality foods from all regions of Italy (olive oil, wine, honey, pasta, rice, desserts, charcuterie, cheeses, preserves, seafood).

Gambero Rosso
www.gamberorosso.it
Fascinating Italian gastronomic website—books, food, wine, events and more.

The Italian Trade Commission
33 E 67th Street
New York, NY 10021
www.italianmade.com
The US official site of the foods and wines of Italy. Includes how to eat Italian-style, where to eat and buy Italian produce in the US, history, and lore of Italian foods and wines.

www.italianwinereview.com
Interesting and impartial news and information about Italian wines.

Wine-Searcher
www.wine-searcher.com
Search engine for finding local importers of Italian wines in the US.

Penzeys Spices
800-741-7787
www.penzeys.com
Penzeys Spice offers more than 250 herbs, spices, and seasonings, including blue poppyseeds, white, green, or pink peppercorns, white and green cardamom, and premium saffron. Shop online, request a catalog, or explore any one of the 39 Penzeys Spice shops nationwide.

Zingerman's
620 Phoenix Drive,
Ann Arbor, Michigan 48108
888-636-8162 or 734-663-DELI
422 Detroit Street
Ann Arbor, Michigan 48104
www.zingermans.com
What began in 1982 as small deli with great sandwiches has grown to a global foods paradise. Zingerman's selection of cheeses, estate-bottled olive oils, and varietal vinegars is unmatched. Their website and catalog are packed with information.

FISH

Browne Trading Company
Merrill's Wharf
260 Commercial Street
Portland, Maine 04101
1-800-944-7848
www.brownetrading.com
Mail-order source for superb fresh fish and shellfish, caviar, and smoked salmon.

Gilmore's Sea Foods
129 Court Street
Bath, Maine
1-800-849-9667
www.gilmoreseafood.com

index

a

agnello, carciofi e olive nere, risotto con, 102
anatra con spinaci, risotto all', 84
arancine di riso, 134
artichokes
    artichoke and pecorino risotto, 45
    risotto with lamb, artichokes, black olives, and garlic, 102
arugula
    spinach risotto with arugula and roasted tomatoes, 26
asparagi con uovo in camicia e parmigiano, risotto agli, 41
asparagus
    asparagus risotto with a poached egg and Parmesan, 41
    spring risotto with herbs, 54

b

barbabietole con radicchio arrostito, risotto con, 30
barlotto with red wine and mushrooms, 129
barolo, risotto al, 58
beef
    risotto with meat sauce, 101
    broth, 19
beet risotto with broiled radicchio, 30
bianco, risotto in, 11–13
black risotto, 107
broccoli risotto with spareribs, 93
broccoli a modo mio, risotto con, 93
brodo di cacciagione, 16
brodo di manzo o vitello, 19
brodo di pesce, 20
brodo di pollo, 16
brodo leggero di frutti di mare, 20
brodo vegetale, 15
budini di riso con amarene e mandorle, 137
butternut squash
    butternut squash, sage, and chile risotto, 33
    pumpkin and pea risotto, 34

c

calamari, risotto bianco con, 108
capers
    caper risotto with grilled tuna and salmoriglio sauce, 123
    chicken liver risotto with Vin Santo, 83
capesante e cipollotti, risotto con, 116
capperi, tonno e salmoriglio, risotto con, 123

caprino, aglio dorato e rosmarino, risotto con, 72
caramelized carrot risotto with watercress pesto, 49
carciofi e pecorino, risotto ai, 45
carote arrostite e pesto al crescione, risotto con, 49
carrots
    caramelized carrot risotto with watercress pesto, 49
    spring risotto with herbs, 54
cheese, 8
    arancine di riso, 134
    artichoke and pecorino risotto, 45
    asparagus risotto with a poached egg and Parmesan, 41
    beet risotto with broiled radicchio, 30
    creamy radicchio and mascarpone risotto, 57
    Gorgonzola and ricotta risotto with crisp sage leaves, 68
    mozzarella and sunblushed tomato risotto with basil, 67
    Parmesan and butter risotto, 63
    pesto risotto, 25
    raclette or Fontina risotto with bresaola, 71
    rice croquettes with tomato sauce, 130
    roasted garlic risotto with goat cheese and rosemary, 72
cherry and almond risotto puddings, 137
chicken
    chicken and mushroom risotto with tarragon, 80
    chicken confit risotto, 79
    light chicken broth, 16
chicken liver risotto with Vin Santo, 83
chiles
    butternut squash, sage, and chile risotto, 33
    crab and chile risotto, 112
chocolate
    dark chocolate risotto, 139
clams
    clam risotto, 120
    seafood risotto, 111
coniglio alla cacciatora, risotto con, 88
cozze o ostriche affumicate, risotto con, 119
cozze o vongole, risotto con, 120
crab and chile risotto, 112
cranberry beans

salami and cranberry bean risotto, 97
croquettes with tomato sauce, 130

d

duck risotto with wilted spinach, 84

e

eggplant
    oven-roasted Mediterranean vegetable risotto, 42
eggs
    asparagus risotto with a poached egg and Parmesan, 41
    truffled egg risotto, 75
erbe verdi e limone, risotto alle, 46

f

fagiano e chianti, risotto al, 87
fegatini e vin santo, risotto ai, 83
fennel and black olive risotto, 50
finocchi con olivere nere, risotto ai, 50
fish broth, 20
frutti di mare, risotto ai, 111

g

game broth, 16
garlic
    risotto with lamb, artichokes, black olives, and garlic, 102
    roasted garlic risotto with goat cheese and rosemary, 72
gelato di riso, 140
goat cheese, roasted garlic risotto with rosemary and, 72
Gorgonzola and ricotta risotto with crisp sage leaves, 68
gorgonzola, ricotta e salvia, risotto al, 68
granchio e peperoncino, risotto al, 112
green beans
    spring risotto with herbs, 54
green herb risotto with white wine and lemon, 46

h

ham
    ham and leek risotto, 98
    rice croquettes with tomato sauce, 130
herbs
    green herb risotto with white wine and lemon, 46
    spring risotto with herbs, 54
hunter's-style rabbit risotto, 88

i

ice cream, rice, 140
Italian sausages and roasted onions, risotto with, 94

l

lamb
    risotto with lamb, artichokes, black olives, and garlic, 102
leeks
    ham and leek risotto with roasted garlic, 98
    smoked mussel or oyster and leek risotto, 119
lemon, green herb risotto with white wine and, 46
lobster risotto, 115

m

mascarpone
    creamy radicchio and mascarpone risotto, 57
meat sauce, risotto with, 101
Mediterranean vegetable risotto, 42
mozzarella and sunblushed tomato risotto with basil, 67
mozzarella e pomodori semi secchi, risotto con, 67
mushrooms
    barlotto with red wine and mushrooms, 129
    chicken and mushroom risotto with tarragon, 80
    hunter's-style rabbit risotto, 88
    wild mushroom risotto, 38
mussels
    mussel risotto, 120
    seafood risotto, 111
    smoked mussel and leek risotto, 119

o

olives
    fennel and black olive risotto, 50
    hunter's-style rabbit risotto, 88
    risotto with lamb, artichokes, black olives, and garlic, 102
orzotto al vino rosso e funghi, 129
oven-roasted Mediterranean vegetable risotto, 42
oysters
    smoked oyster and leek risotto, 119

p

pancetta
    creamy radicchio and mascarpone risotto, 57

duck risotto with wilted spinach, 84
little tomato risotto cakes, 133
pancetta e porri, risotto con, 98
Parmesan and butter risotto, 63
parmigiana, risotto alla, 63
pearl barley
  barlotto with red wine and mushrooms, 129
peas
  pumpkin and pea risotto, 34
  spring risotto with herbs, 54
  Venetian pea and rice thick soup, 53
pesto
  caramelized carrot risotto with watercress pesto, 49
  pesto risotto, 25
pesto, risotto al, 25
pheasant and red wine risotto, 87
pollo conservato, risotto al, 79
pollo, funghi e dragoncello, risotto al, 80
pomodori, risotto ai tre, 29
pork
  broccoli risotto with spare ribs, 93
  risotto with meat sauce, 101
primavera alle erbe, risotto, 54
pumpkin
  butternut squash, sage, and chile risotto, 33
  pumpkin and pea risotto, 34

r
rabbit
  hunter's-style rabbit risotto, 88
raclette o fontina con bresaola, risotto alla, 71
raclette or Fontina risotto with bresaola, 71
radicchio
  beet risotto with broiled radicchio, 30
  creamy radicchio and mascarpone risotto, 57
radicchio e mascarpone, risotto cremoso al, 57
ragù
  arancine di riso, 134
  risotto with meat sauce, 101
ragù, risotto al, 101
relish, black olive and fennel, 50
rice
  cultivation, 7
  storing, 8
  varieties, 7–8

ricotta
  Gorgonzola and ricotta risotto with crisp sage leaves, 68
risi e bisi, 53
riso nero, 139
rosemary, roasted garlic risotto with goat cheese and, 72

s
saffron
  saffron risotto, 64
salame e fagioli borlotti, risotto con, 97
salami and cranberry bean risotto, 97
salsicce e cipolle arrostite, risotto con, 94
salmone affumicato, risotto cremoso con, 124
saltimbocca di risotto, 133
sausages
  risotto with Italian sausages and roasted onions, 94
scallions
  scallop and scallion risotto, 116
scallops
  scallop and spring onion risotto, 116
  seafood risotto, 111
seafood risotto, 111
seafood broth, 20
seppie, risotto al nero di, 107
shrimp
  shrimp risotto, 115
  seafood risotto, 111
smoked mussel or oyster and leek risotto, 119
smoked salmon risotto, 124
spinach
  duck risotto with wilted spinach, 84
  spinach risotto with rocket and roasted tomatoes, 26
spinaci, rucola e pomodori, risotto con, 26
spring risotto with herbs, 54
squash *see* butternut squash
squid
  black risotto, 107
  seafood risotto, 111
  white squid risotto, 108
broths, 8
  beef or veal broth, 19
  fish broth, 20
  game broth, 16
  game broth with wild boar or venison, 19
  light chicken broth, 16
  quick seafood broth, 20

vegetable broth, 15
supplì al telefono con sugo di pomodoro, 130

t
tomatoes
  little tomato risotto cakes, 133
  mozzarella and sunblushed tomato risotto with basil, 67
  rice croquettes with tomato sauce, 130
  risotto with Italian sausages and roasted onions, 94
  risotto with meat sauce, 101
  spinach risotto with arugula and roasted tomatoes, 26
  triple tomato risotto with basil, 29
tre tipi di pomodori, risotto con, 29
truffled egg risotto, 75
tuna
  caper risotto with broiled tuna and salmoriglio sauce, 123

u
uovo e tartufi, risotto all', 75

v
veal
  risotto with meat sauce, 101
  broth, 19
vegetables, 23–59
  oven-roasted Mediterranean vegetable risotto, 42
  broth, 15
  see also individual types of vegetable
Venetian pea and rice thick soup, 53
verdure del mediterraneo, risotto con, 42

w
white risotto step-by-step, 11–13
white squid risotto, 108
wild mushroom risotto, 38

z
zafferano, risotto allo, 64
zucca e piselli, risotto alla, 34
zucca, peperoncino e salvia, risotto alla, 33
zucchine, risotto con fiori di, 37
zucchini
  squash blossom risotto, 37
  oven-roasted Mediterranean vegetable risotto, 42

conversion charts

Weights and measures have been rounded up or down slightly to make measuring easier.

Volume equivalents:

American	Metric	Imperial
1 teaspoon	5 ml	
1 tablespoon	15 ml	
¼ cup	60 ml	2 fl.oz.
⅓ cup	75 ml	2½ fl.oz.
½ cup	125 ml	4 fl.oz.
⅔ cup	150 ml	5 fl.oz. (¼ pint)
¾ cup	175 ml	6 fl.oz.
1 cup	250 ml	8 fl.oz.

Weight equivalents: / **Measurements:**

Imperial	Metric	Inches	cm
1 oz.	25 g	¼ inch	5 mm
2 oz.	50 g	½ inch	1 cm
3 oz.	75 g	¾ inch	1.5 cm
4 oz.	125 g	1 inch	2.5 cm
5 oz.	150 g	2 inches	5 cm
6 oz.	175 g	3 inches	7 cm
7 oz.	200 g	4 inches	10 cm
8 oz. (½ lb.)	250 g	5 inches	12 cm
9 oz.	275 g	6 inches	15 cm
10 oz.	300 g	7 inches	18 cm
11 oz.	325 g	8 inches	20 cm
12 oz.	375 g	9 inches	23 cm
13 oz.	400 g	10 inches	25 cm
14 oz.	425 g	11 inches	28 cm
15 oz.	475 g	12 inches	30 cm
16 oz. (1 lb.)	500 g		
2 lb.	1 kg		

Oven temperatures:

110°C	(225°F)	Gas ¼
120°C	(250°F)	Gas ½
140°C	(275°F)	Gas 1
150°C	(300°F)	Gas 2
160°C	(325°F)	Gas 3
180°C	(350°F)	Gas 4
190°C	(375°F)	Gas 5
200°C	(400°F)	Gas 6
220°C	(425°F)	Gas 7
230°C	(450°F)	Gas 8
240°C	(475°F)	Gas 9